Small Businesses Give Big

Why Charitable Giving is a Great Business Strategy

Edited by Maggie F. Keenan, Ed.D.

December, 2008

A percentage of the proceeds of this book
goes to support
Little Red Wagon Foundation
www.littleredwagonfoundation.com

Small Businesses Give Big

Published by:
Alma Publishing
Dallas, OR
USA

ISBN: 978-0-9796745-5-6

Cover design: Bright White Space, LLC.
Copy editing and book layout: Naomi Pierce, Studio N
Printed in the United States of America

For my dear friend,
Sandra,
for believing in me

Contents

Acknowledgements

I had a friend who always told me that I would write a book one day. But over the years, I never gave it too much thought. I am not so sure my doctoral dissertation was what my friend had in mind at the time. It wasn't until the end of last year that this book idea surfaced.

I knew the timing was right when everything for this book fell into place quickly and effortlessly. The right people showed up to participate and contribute to the chapters, and to support and encourage me through the process. My special thanks to all the business authors represented in each chapter for your willingness to be a part of this book and for your time and effort to write your business giving story. To Donna Kozik, my book coach and sister friend for your mentoring, advice, and constant emails which got me over the humps. To Naomi Pierce for your superior editorial services and Ariel Janzen for your artistic talent and creativity which made this book cover pop.

I also want to express my deep gratitude and love to my mastermind circle: Lisa Buldo (**www.lisabuldo.com**), Heather Dominick (**www.energyrich-coach.com**), Sonia M. Miller (**www.successforthesoul.com**), and Simone Mitjans (**www.purewomenshealth.com**). Our monthly Monday morning calls are the most valuable investment I make to my work with **givingadvice**. Your ideas, inspiration, feedback, and constant support have helped me grow along this journey. You are fabulous women who keep challenging me to stay true to my voice and heart each step of the way. I especially want to thank Lisa Buldo. Your unwavering belief, faith, and strength in God have touched my life.

To all my clients, I am grateful for the opportunities to work with you. Each project allows me to broaden my knowledge, deepen my expertise, and make a difference in the world. My wish is that your charitable giving programs continue to make an impact for your business and for the lives and communities you will touch, whether it's in your corner of this world or across the globe.

And to those who have helped me bring **givingadvice** to the sweet place it is today: Sarah Lamar, Kate Strain, Rob Cordasco, Fabienne Fredrickson, Ali Brown, Loretta Mitchell, and Jenny House.

A special thanks and shout out to my life long girl friends. I am truly blessed to have you in my life: Kim Craig, Teresa Coryell, Kathy McAdoo, Kim Jungkind, Laurel Brady, and Rita Debate, Ph.D. No matter the miles or time, your ears and heart are as if you're in the same room with me.

Finally, to my husband, running partner, confidant, and truly best friend, Mark. You help me to realize that each day is not just a list of things to do or series of accomplishments, but rather something to be enjoyed. I really do listen when you say, "Promise me you'll have some fun today, Mag." I love you and our life together!

Introduction

You've never met me, but because you are reading this book, I know we share something in common — we are business owners and we want to make a difference while making a living. On some level you may be supporting causes. But, you may be thinking to yourself, "I'll give in a bigger way when I have more money to give." If you are waiting until 'later' to give or have the mindset of not having enough to give now, you are missing out on rewarding opportunities to make a difference right now.

I am here to tell you that it doesn't matter if you've been in business for six months or six years, or if you make $50,000 or $500,000; the defining moment is now. All it takes is the heart to help, passion to fuel your purpose, and the decision to make giving an integral part of your business.

You are about to read amazing stories of business owners just like you who have made a conscious decision to make giving an important part of their business. I asked them to share their stories and describe the value giving has in their businesses. Each giving story reflects their passion, purpose, and wealth of spirit. Within the following pages you will find a wide spectrum of giving. Each one is unique and an expression of the personal influences in their lives. The giving stories are not like the formal way of giving back where a committee sits around a board room table and reads proposals and decides how much to give to which charities, and where giving has had little or no connection to business principles. And forget making giving fun and engaging. See, writing a check is an easy thing to do. As a matter of fact, I always say that is the easiest way to give and the easiest part of giving. Giving is a value that goes beyond the simple task of cutting checks. It requires engaging, caring, serving, and reaching out to help others. From here giving is done with a sense of purpose and commitment toward serving a local community or a place on the other side of the world. In each chapter, an ethical and moral principle served as the backbone and unique characteristic of the business. By aligning their values with their business, these business owners show us how giving and business growth are inextricably linked, and they have had fun along the way, feeling the joy giving has brought them.

Within these stories, you will hear the voices of business owners who are second generation family-owned businesses, solo entrepreneurs who have followed their passion, and partnerships that emerged from friendships. No one business is the same. They differ in their size, services and products, revenues, industry, location, and the way they give back. Yet, they share some common characteristics:

They have a deep sense of purpose to help their community.

Collectively, the business owners in this book are compassionate individuals. They each serve a community and they give to the causes in their community. Some broadened their giving across the globe. But, regardless of whether we define community by geographic boundaries or by spheres of influence, it is the purpose we are committed to that is defining and determines success and impact.

Their business giving is a reflection of their values.

Not surprisingly, we know that the essence of who we are defines our business, and the stories in this book are excellent examples of how individual or family values are truly connected to the company's values. Their values developed the business's giving which is deeply ingrained in its foundation. Integrating your values—that which you stand for without sway—into business activities, decisions, and principles is surrendering to who you are and living and working consciously from those beliefs. When you do this, success flows.

They made giving a part of their business from the get-go.

The idea that giving can be a part of a business from the very beginning may be unusual, particularly when new business owners are putting in countless hours and managing every aspect of business just to keep it going. When you throw a giving program into the mix, you have to wonder how you would have the time and effort to put towards managing giving. That is exactly what these business owners did. Whether they are a second-generation family business owner or a solo entrepreneur, giving was a part of the business from the beginning. Their giving evolved and grew as business has, and their passion fueled their commitment to keeping giving as an important aspect of the business.

They let the rewards of giving spill back into the business without seeking the results.

There is truth in the saying, "What you give is the measure of what you receive." But somewhere in there lies the notion that the intentions to give must be pure and without seeking anything in return. This sounds like a moral truth and it is. And while you may not be a particularly spiritual person, know this: that if you set out to build a giving program for the sole purpose of building and growing your business it will not happen. Flat out, it will not happen. The stories in this book reflect the karmic return of their giving on their business and for them personally. Not one of them set out to give to in order to 'get.' They give because they know it is the right thing to do. The positive effects on their business are simply the rewards for acting with pure intention.

This is not a how-to book, a step-by-step guide to giving, or a standard set of questions that each business owner answered. Rather, it is their stories from their own hearts. This is a book that shows you how meaningful a giving program can be for businesses and how businesses and causes both benefit at the end of the day. It tells you through personal experiences and real-life stories because this is how we connect with one another and how we are inspired to do something different, learn, and grow.

My hope is that you will be inspired as you read each chapter of this book and that you make a connection with one or more of these business giving programs and see the possibilities of how you can make an impact in your own community. These are stories of business owners making an extraordinary difference in their own backyard. There are always environmental issues to be solved, individuals and families who need a leg up, and diseases that need a cure. Meeting these needs takes people and businesses that are passionate enough to help solve them. Business giving programs don't have to be administrative-aside projects, but rather a rich opportunity to grow your business, to make a meaningful connection to your community, and to champion for cause.

CHAPTER

1

Seattle Chocolate Company

Chick and Extreme Chocolates Raise Thousands for Breast Cancer Research

Jean Thompson, chief executive officer and owner of Seattle Chocolate Company, began giving back in a huge way just 3 years after being thrust into the driver's seat of the 16-year-old Seattle-based chocolate maker.

Founded in 1992, Seattle Chocolate makes premium chocolate under beloved brands such as Frangos and Choxie for major retailers, and sells chocolate under its own name and own lines, including Chick Chocolates, through retailers around the country.

A former marketing executive for Microsoft Corp., Thompson and her husband Rick invested in Seattle Chocolate in 1998 and were silent partners for several years.

When the chocolate company started to falter in late 2002, Thompson stepped in to help — after spending 11 years as a stay-at-home mom. She quickly found herself in charge not 6 weeks later upon the unexpected departure of Seattle Chocolate's long time CEO.

Thompson quickly switched into high gear and tapped into her marketing and advertising knowledge. She implemented changes she hoped would make the company healthy again. She expanded the company's territory, marketed Seattle Chocolates to major stores such as Target Corp. and Macy's, and began marketing their products as everyday chocolate — not just a holiday treat.

As she experimented with packaging and marketing strategies, Thompson struck gold: Most women eat chocolate daily, so why not design a product line for women? Thompson ran with this idea, launching her Chick Chocolates line in June 2004.

The Chicks are small treasures wrapped in sassy packaging. The boxes are thin, mimicking a lipstick case. Each contains 3 individually wrapped truffles, allowing women to control their portions. The initial line consisted of three types of chocolate: Strong Chick, a calcium-fortified milk chocolate; Extreme Chick, a dark chocolate blended with cocoa nibs; and Nutty Chick, a blend of milk chocolate, toffee and almonds. The line was an instant hit, and sales soared.

Fast forward 4 years and Seattle Chocolate Company now boasts sales of $10 million and climbing. Thompson has added to the company's workforce significantly, and the company has expanded its facilities to include a 65,000 square foot production and warehouse facility.

A Call to Action

As the company started to once again fire on all cylinders, Thompson was hit with a huge, personal scare. During a routine visit to the doctor, she was told she had a suspicious lump in her breast, which could be cancer.

The then 45-year-old Thompson had already lost her aunt and mother-in-law to breast cancer. Her aunt and mother were very close, and her aunt's death had a big impact on Thompson's extended family. "What will this do to my daughter?" Thompson worried as she waited to find out the results of her tests. Thompson's daughter was just 9 at the time.

"This was a very emotional time," Thompson said of the nearly two weeks it took to get her test results. "On the day of resolution, I went into the marketing department and said regardless of my results, we're doing something for breast cancer research."

Luckily for Thompson, her test results were negative for cancer. But the ordeal made a lasting impact. "Someone out there didn't get the happy news that I did," she said. "You spend all your spare time worrying 'What If?' We need to get rid of breast cancer; it affects too many babies and women and it's not okay."

Thompson's daughter has the genetic lineage for breast cancer and if Thompson can play even a small role in helping to find a cure in order to make sure her daughter and future grandchildren are not lost to cancer, she's willing to try.

"I watched my aunt struggle for 9 years and it's a horrible way to go," she said. "If there's any way I can keep my daughter from suffering like that, I'm going to try."

Finding a Partner

Coming up with a way to support breast cancer research was easy. Seattle Chocolate added a fourth Chick to the new women's line, naming her Survivor Chick. Survivor Chick is a dark chocolate truffle with a white chocolate and all natural raspberry flavored center. One hundred percent of the profits from the sale of Survivor Chick go to organizations that support research to prevent women's cancers.

"I realized I am fortunate enough to be able to do something, while a lot of other women want to do something, but can't," said Thompson, referring to her position as a company owner and chief executive.

"It's so much more powerful and leveraged to give women (or anyone) who loves chocolate the ability to give back and contribute in a small way than it is to depend on a small few writing big checks," Thompson added.

Sales of the Survivor Chick allowed Seattle Chocolates to donate $8,400 to Athena Partners in 2007. But Thompson knew the bar could be raised.

Too "Pink" Limits Sales

"The Chicks were super well received and profiled on The Food Network, but because of the pink-ribboned packaging, the Survivor Chick became a seasonal item taken in by retailers only during the breast cancer awareness month of October," she said. "It was limiting the amount we could raise."

"It really annoyed me. People are fighting cancer every day and the research needs to be funded every month of the year, not just October."

So it became Thompson's mission to figure out how she could get consumers to help every day. The solution presented itself instantly. Why not tweak the packaging on one of her best-selling truffle bars, which were already carried all year and nationwide? The entire line is available in well over 12,000 retail, grocery, and drug stores across the nation and via the company's online store.

"Our Extreme Dark Truffle Bar is already dressed in hot pink packaging, so we added a tiny pink ribbon on the back so consumers know they are helping with the fight, but retailers view it as an everyday item and carry it year round. Because our Extreme Dark bar starts with 65 percent cacao dark chocolate and dark chocolate is starting to overtake milk chocolate in popularity in the US, the bar promises to significantly accelerate our giving."

The packaging for the entire 10-bar Truffle Bar line was redesigned recently. The Extreme Dark Truffle Bar and other bars are brightly colored and carry bold graphics. The pink ribbon underneath the Extreme Dark Truffle Bar is a treat each consumer can discover as she enjoys the dark chocolate she purchases, and is something she can feel good about — knowing she is helping future women win the battle against breast cancer.

"We aren't broadcasting that message," said Thompson. "We don't want retailers to view the bar as a "Breast Cancer Awareness month" product but rather carry them all year round. Let's face it; women eat chocolate year round, not just in October."

Sassy Packaging Has Power to Raise Millions

The sassy new packaging has caught the attention of Oprah Winfrey, whose team featured the Extreme Dark Truffle Bar and truffle bar line within the "Love That" section of the October 2008 issue of *O* Magazine. Thompson and the Extreme Dark Truffle Bar were also featured in the November 2008 issue of *More* Magazine and the December 2008 issue of *Success* Magazine. Such powerful attention is bringing the company and the product to the awareness of millions of chocolate-loving women who may likely enjoy it more knowing that every purchase does something wonderful to help find a cure for women's cancers.

"Regardless of the positive attention powerful magazines like *O*, *More*, and *Success* can bring, our commitment is sure and everlasting," said Thompson.

Seattle Chocolate Company also donates chocolate to many charities and school groups. Because their products are so desirable and company executives are inundated with requests, Thompson and her team have created a giving policy to keep their giving manageable. The company focuses on charities associated with women, children, and education.

Thompson was recently elected to a three-year term to serve on the Board of Trustees for the National Confectionery Association. She has been named a finalist in the 2008 Nellie Cashman Woman Business Owner of the Year award in recognition of her pioneering spirit and commitment to community. Prior to taking the helm at Seattle Chocolate Company, Thompson volunteered time, talent, and leadership by serving on the board of the Boys and Girls Club, the planning commission for Yarrow Point, and the Task Force for the Gifted Program for the Bellevue School District. She also served a number of tours of duty as room parent for her children Danny and Ellie during their elementary and middle school years.

"Running the chocolate company has given me the best opportunity of my life to give back to society," Thompson added. "In addition to the cancer research donation program, I'm helping 75 families keep their heads above water by providing jobs. There's nothing I could have possibly done during all my years volunteering that would have had this meaningful of an impact on so many people. While Seattle Chocolate is not a non-profit organization, by creating and growing a strong company I can make a significant impact on my extended family here."

— **Nancy S. Juetten**, on behalf of Seattle Chocolate Company CEO **Jean Thompson**

Seattle Chocolate Company manufactures premium 100 percent, all natural truffles, truffle bars, dessert shells, and chocolates under the Seattle Chocolates and Chick Chocolates brands, along with a wide range of private label brands. While the art of fine chocolate is the company's undeniable passion, the biggest thrill is being able to share Seattle Chocolates with customers and have fun along the way. Seattle Chocolate Company uses the finest European chocolate and the purest, 100 percent all-natural flavorings. Blending together the world's highest-quality ingredients, expert chocolatiers craft a meltaway masterpiece that satisfies like no other. Seattle Chocolate Company products are beautifully packaged in stunning gift boxes and bags. Luxuriously smooth, unique, kosher-certified, 100 percent all-natural truffles are tasteful treats you can feel good about giving and enjoying every day. Learn more at **www.seattlechocolates.com**.

Contact Information

Nancy S. Juetten, 425-641-5214, **nancy@nsjmktg.com**
Jean Thompson, 425-264-2800, **Jean@seachoco.com**

CHAPTER

2

Melaver, Inc.

Giving Back as a Fundamental Business Model for Stewards of Land and Community

"Depression-era business people," my father liked to say, "fall into one of two camps. There are those who, growing up with very little, are determined to hoard everything they earned so as never to go hungry again. And there are those who, remembering what it was like to be hungry themselves, give generously to others who should never experience such deprivations."

My family and our business practices fall into the latter category. It has been that way for three generations. At its core, the notion of giving back carries with it a fundamental recognition that where we are in life, who we have become, the paths in life that have opened up before us, are not because we have made it on our own, but because we have been afforded opportunities owing to an entire system that has selflessly paved the way for us — a system comprised of both nature and society, land and community.

A little background is called for here. Melaver, Inc., the sustainable real estate company I run based in Savannah, Georgia, has its roots in a corner grocery store my grandmother, Annie Melaver, founded in 1940. Even back then, when she owned a foundling business, my grandmother, a hard-nosed business woman in many ways, made little distinction between selling groceries and servicing the neighborhood in which her corner store was located. Many of her customers bought on credit, paying only when and if they could. She would occasionally close the store to bring soup to a neighbor who was ill.

My father, Norton Melaver, joined his mother in the store after he graduated from college and expanded the business over the ensuing 40 years to a supermarket chain in and around Savannah. He too was a sharp businessman. But the same ethos of blurring the lines between growing a business and serving the community held sway. Some of the profits from the store were always given back to others, primarily the small Jewish community of which we were a part. We participated in a local workman's circle credit union, established primarily as a Jewish revolving loan fund in which Jewish businesses provided interest-optional seed funds to others. My father, his sister Millie, and my mother Betty Stein Melaver all gave time and funds to various civic organizations, Jewish and non-Jewish alike. An early and pervasive memory of my childhood were the ongoing meetings that took place in our home after my sisters and I had gone to bed. Business, family, and civic engagement back then were not separate spheres of life but deeply intertwined with one another.

In 1985, we sold the family grocery business but held on to the various real estate holdings that comprised the business: some shopping centers, a few warehouses, and an office of sorts. It was a defining moment in many ways; several points are worth dwelling on here. For one, about 6 percent of the proceeds of the sale of the business were distributed to employees of the company who had worked for us for at least a year. Secondly, about another 8 percent was set aside to create a foundation to address ongoing needs in the community. Finally, the sale of the grocery business set in motion a family debate about the nascent real estate company we suddenly found ourselves running. How did we feel about real estate? Not great, given general practices that stripped the land of trees, designed projects that made one town look indistinguishable from all others, and, in general, degenerated water and air quality, promoted gross inefficiencies in our use of resources, tied us ever more insidiously to gross use of fossil fuels, and eviscerated a sense of community. We wanted, if we were going to stay in real estate, to do real estate a different way, one in which we would be stewards of both land and community. Thus began our evolution into a sustainable real estate business, one in which we have been passionately involved for nearly two decades.

The image or metaphor I most like to draw on to capture our 70-year history is that of a pond of water, where a pebble creates a rippling effect outward across the surface of the water. As the ripples expand, the extent of our engagement with others in the community also increases. So too do our circles of engagement with an ever-increasing set of stakeholders and issues. At the very center of this series of concentric circles is a notion of business that ensures its own health and viability by participating in the health and viability of the larger contexts of which it is a part. That, I feel, is the central purpose of a business. A business cannot sustain itself for the long term unless it serves as a trustee of the contexts around it.

So in the early years of our company, the notion of giving back was largely personal or familial and centered around a neighborhood, a tribe (the Jewish community), and volunteer work in various civic organizations. Time, professional knowledge, and money (the old standard of work, wisdom, and wealth) comprised the scrip in this exchange. As we have evolved, the locus of giving has broadened — to include virtually all staff members working in the business as well as other close, outside vendors and partners — and the nature of giving has been extended. Our company now sponsors programs to help realize the highest potential of our staff, provides educational outreach into the community and beyond (particularly on issues related to sustainability), shares professional knowledge with others (pro bono consulting), has founded or participates in non-profits linked to issues central to company values (sustainability, social welfare, education), engages in political advocacy, and gets involved in community projects.

The choice of people who work for our company, the on-going emphasis on making work a sphere of life where one can find personal meaning and realize one's highest potential, the activities all staff members engage in to integrate work with other aspects of their lives, the projects we choose to develop: all of these are facets of a business deeply integrated into community, where the lines between the dancer and the dance, as it were, become so blurred that the notion of giving back itself seems overly linear, falling far shy of what a business is capable of. A graphic representation of this expanding sense of giving back can be seen in Figure 1.

Figure 1. Expanding the Circles of Giving

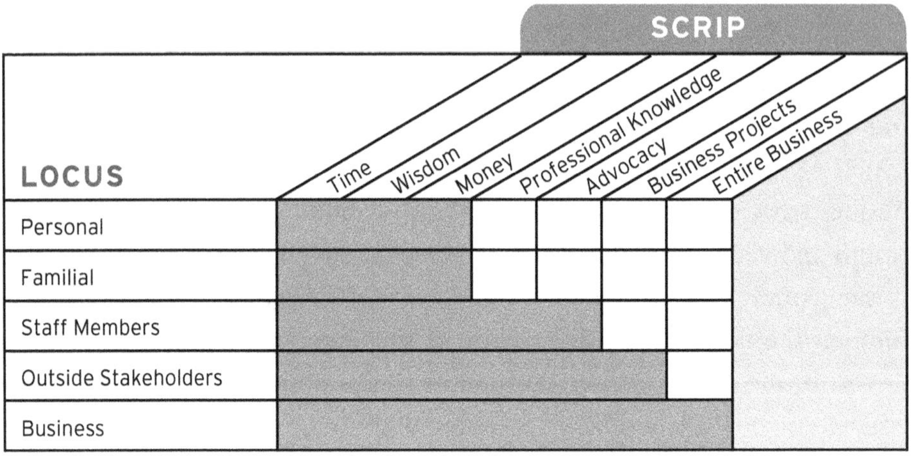

SCRIP

LOCUS	Time	Wisdom	Money	Professional Knowledge	Advocacy	Business Projects	Entire Business
Personal							
Familial							
Staff Members							
Outside Stakeholders							
Business							

What prompts a company such as ours to build its entire business model around a notion of giving back? Can it be profitable doing so? Is this particular model replicable by other businesses? Is it scalable or is such a model limited to smaller companies such as our own?

The core values at the heart of our company: do right, learn, serve, profit — core values I might add that all staff members at Melaver, Inc. worked on collectively for about a year before total agreement was reached — serve as a key driver of what we do and how we do it. It has been a key focus of our business to optimize financial, social, and environmental returns (the triple bottom-line) rather than maximize profits. It is our belief, deeply held, that business simply cannot be practiced on a dead planet and that it is in business's own self-interest to be better stewards of land and community.

Imagine planning your business for the long term and anticipating that 40 percent of the world will be facing chronic water shortages by 2025. Or that by 2050, our carbon emissions could be at 600 parts per million or higher, a level unknown in human history. Or that 20 years from now, our current daily consumption of 85 million barrels of oil per day is likely to increase 40 percent. Or that we are consuming 25 million acres of land every year for real estate development while arable land is decreasing and food production on remaining agricultural lands is becoming ever more chemical and fossil dependent. Consider at least for a minute your own company's long-term strategic plan and ask yourself this, what would happen to that strategic plan if one or two basic assumptions underlying your company's thinking were to go wildly astray? And then consider this, what alternative vision of your business might you begin to construct to account for such challenges to your business's strategic assumptions?

The key challenges for us as a company over the years have been: 1) to understand better the inseparable links between humankind and nature; 2) to enhance our understanding of how land planning, growth management, water quality and quantity, air quality, and energy efficiency are interrelated; and 3) to ratchet up our coordination with the various other sectors of society — government, non-profits, and academic institutions — to address these large systemic issues more effectively. At its core, our business plan relies on a fundamental capacity to integrate and coordinate: to see the connectivity among the various aspects of our lives and to foster greater integrative thought and behavior through the coordinated efforts of a citizenry. We don't conduct business on the one hand and give back on the other. The two actions are actually one and the same.

That approach has also been profitable. It would have to be, otherwise our own capacity to sustain our business would be short-lived. In *The Green Building Bottom Line,* a book co-written by colleagues and close outside partners, we provide a lengthy analysis of how a business model focused on doing good in the community can also do well financially. How well? We estimate an annual return on our investments in sustainable practices to be around 30 percent. Significant portions of that return have to do with attracting and retaining people, projects, and capital, all desiring to be part of a mission-driven endeavor. Tellingly, for a long time we had no idea that our notion of fusing business with giving back would have such a payoff. We simply embarked on a path we felt was right.

Those returns have enabled us in recent years to communicate an important message to the business community generally: this model is not only replicable and scalable, it is one that a business ignores at its peril. There are numerable signs that the marketplace generally is demanding that business either hold itself — or be held — to a higher moral standard of conduct. We cannot, for instance, continue to outsource jobs and the carbon emissions that go with those jobs and expect not to feel the negative consequences of those actions. My hometown of Savannah, as a result of that outsourcing of jobs and emissions, is projected to be underwater before the end of this century. The old, untenable model is an "away" model: a notion that we can externalize our effects on society and nature by sending those costs elsewhere. The new model recognizes that there is no such thing as "away," that we live in a closed system. The new business model is a "here" model in which business focuses on its footprint on nature and society, a model in which giving back is also a gift — a gift of survival — to the business itself.

At ground level, our company's various giving back activities can seem confusing and chaotic. At any given moment, some staff members will be engaged in continuing education while others are speaking to groups about sustainable practices. Some will form an action coalition in the community to promote city-wide recycling while others are helping the county develop a comprehensive green program. We donate to various local, regional, and state causes such as The Georgia Conservancy. We partner with the Savannah Tree Foundation to plant trees throughout the community as part of an effort to combine beautification with carbon sequestration. We donate compact fluorescent bulbs to non-profits. We work closely with a neighborhood association and the local housing authority to create sustainable affordable housing. At a bird's-eye level, these various efforts coalesce, shaping an entire business model around enhancing the quality of life for our society while reducing our impact upon nature.

The 12th century Judaic scholar and philosopher Maimonides developed a hierarchy of eight levels of giving, beginning with a contribution that is provided grudgingly when one is approached directly by a person in need and culminating in an anonymous act of setting someone up in business so that he or she is no longer dependent on others. Perhaps a ninth level of giving should be added to this schema, one in which the very nature of business itself reduces need.

—Martin Melaver

Melaver, Inc. is a third-generation family-owned business devoted solely to sustainable principles and practices. Embracing a triple bottom-line approach to all its activities, the company's purpose is to envelop the community in a fabric of innovative, sustainable, inspiring practices. Melaver has garnered numerous awards for its cutting-edge sustainable projects, and is considered a leader in the sustainability movement in the United States.

The company develops, constructs, renovates, owns and manages both commercial and residential real estate holdings and provides a full set of services that complement its work: construction and development, consultancy, brokerage, asset management, property management. Project experience ranges across all major real estate product types: retail, office, hotel, industrial, home, and multi-family residential.

Contact Information

Melaver, Inc.
114 Barnard St., Ste. 2B
Savannah, GA 31401
www.melaver.com

CHAPTER 3

Alexandria Brown International, Inc.

Giving and Finding Freedom for Herself & Others

Giving in the Beginning

Like many of us growing up, I didn't have a distinct role model for giving back. It's not something most families discuss around the dinner table, and I didn't know wealthy people, let alone those who put philanthropy into practice. In fact, although it's not quite "giving back," most of us are familiar with having to sell products for organizations, and I was among the legions of Girl Scouts selling cookies. What I experienced was that it always seemed to irritate people when you asked for money, with the rare exception of the one person who would buy 20 boxes of cookies. (God bless them!)

I remember when I started working for companies in New York and people would come around asking for support with fundraising projects. Everyday it seemed like it was someone asking for something. I dreaded it because I never had money for them. Also, before I understood the energy of money and the power of giving back, I even felt a little bothered they would ask — couldn't they see I was barely making ends meet already? So, again, like many of us, those were my first experiences about giving —not extremely positive.

After starting my own business, I began to understand more how the energy of money works and how the energy needs to circulate. Plus, some charities knew exactly how to get to me. Since I'm a big animal lover, whenever I received those letters in the mail with a picture of a sad puppy, it broke my heart. I couldn't whip out my checkbook fast enough! I even used the direct mail pieces as marketing examples to my followers — those letters were that good! Yes, it was only $25 here and there; however, it was a fair amount to me since my business was nowhere near the level it is now.

Later, I started to better understand how putting money back out into the world would actually help my flow coming in. I've come to realize that this is a very important concept. As time went on, I realized that if I did something great like help a cause I'm passionate about, it would actually come back to me just by the reciprocal nature of the Universe.

Party for a Cause

In 2005, a number of things came together to take my giving to a new level. I was about to have my very first seminar. At the same time, I was also planning a huge birthday party. No one seemed to have good parties anymore, and I thought, "I want to have a really good party!" I was brainstorming with some colleagues at the front of the room with a flip chart, where I had the party on one side, the workshop on the other and, in another section, ideas for a fundraiser.

One of my friends pointed at the chart and said, "Why don't you do them all together?" I looked at it a second and shouted, "Wow, can I do that?" It was a real "eureka!" moment. The whole project then took on a great energy, and on the last night of the seminar, I hosted a birthday bash on a party yacht in Marina Del Rey.

I paid for the party and then charged $100 a ticket to make it a fundraiser for the Humane Society of the United States. Everyone had a great time, and we gave the Humane Society a check for $10,000.

It was such a success that 2 years later I did the same thing. We had even more people, made it a fun '80s-themed party, and raised $15,000 for the Make-A-Wish Foundation. We not only did fundraising for two worthy organizations, but also we created a greater awareness for social causes. Plus we got to boogie down!

Others' Reactions — Good & Bad

Although I like to think my actions inspire others to give, when I started sharing openly about the funds I was raising and giving back, I had a few people who follow me write some very "interesting" things — everyone suddenly had an opinion about me and what charities I was supporting. They wrote, "You think you're so special giving this back. You probably have a lot more money to give." And, "Why did you pick *that* charity? You should have picked *this* charity."

It stung a little bit, but I was determined to stay true to my message. When I shared with others what I was doing, I wasn't saying "You have to give to this particular charity." I said, "We can all do this. We can all do this together." I share my stories of what I'm doing to inspire others. And I really don't care if people know I give back or not. I'm being true to myself and the social responsibility I feel to others; that doesn't include explaining my actions.

The reason I share with people that I'm giving back is so it inspires others to say, "Let's all do this in our own way. I can throw a party like she did. I can give a percentage of my product or service, or I can do something that gives my time." It's more about that wonderful energy moving from one person to another.

When others start talking that way, my energy increases. That's the flow of energy that is so powerful about giving back — it grows and expands and, to me, is the purest form of philanthropy.

The Power of Giving and Receiving

For other business owners looking to give back and grow their businesses, I suggest a three-tiered approach. First, start with what you can, whether it's helping out the fundraising student knocking at the front door or writing a check to the employee who's participating in a race to cure Muscular Dystrophy. Next, be "open to opening up." I remember when I held on so tightly, money wouldn't come in. Then I started letting go and saw money was energy, and it flows and comes back. Finally, I believe it's true that the more you give, the more your business will grow. It's that simple, yet it has to be experienced to be believed.

My business has taken 10 years to build, and my giving has grown right along with it. I had many years when I had no money and was broke. I do feel very blessed, and I've worked very hard for it. Now I give for the joy of giving. I feel no obligation or guilt that drives me to give and feel, ideally, this is the way it should be. It's more empowering to both the giver and the receiver.

I receive when I give. I receive emotionally, and I have found that I also receive financially. What goes around comes around. And I think giving *should* be from choice rather than guilt or obligation. That's why there is joy in it!

Giving Back Creates a Thriving Business

Today, I have become very clear on what I want to accomplish in this lifetime and how to use my business as a vehicle for that. Giving is one of those channels where I can make a difference with my business.

With my company, Alexandria Brown International, I'm moving on to the next level of giving. I've had some great conversations with leaders from Virgin Unite, which is Virgin's philanthropic arm. I was very grateful to spend time with Richard Branson on his private island in the Caribbean, and I am now looking into ways to incorporate some of their efforts, which would blend nicely with my business.

I have taken an interest in women's issues around the world. I'm doing a lot of research right now on microloans for women. My vision is that by giving more women financial power, there will be more peace in the world.

I feel very strongly about this. Women around the world aren't the ones fighting over land and killing each other. We just want to keep everyone fed, happy, and living a beautiful life. The more women we can help step up and claim their power, the more we will feel that shift start happening—we'll start changing the world.

And it's not just about the money. It's also about the support I can offer the women striving to improve themselves and grow their businesses here, such as when I offer someone a scholarship to one of my seminars. I like to make little gestures like that when appropriate and when it can make a big difference. I've also given some consultations and conversations to women wanting some direction about what they can do to succeed. It's not about selling them anything or urging them to come to one of my events. Instead it's about having a one-on-one discussion and giving support and encouragement to another. It's empowering knowing I can change a woman's life simply by having a conversation with her.

And I aim high! Someone who is a very big inspiration to me is Oprah and her "Big Give." I like how she's raising people's awareness of what they can do. That's the level of magnitude I want to be at for giving. I want to get people involved in the giving. Plus, I think the most significant contribution I have made is still coming — I like to think things are shifting so my contributions are more and more impactful, and each one tops the one before.

The beautiful thing about being a business owner is we build a platform for ourselves. We have a lot of publicity. We have a lot of access to media. Why not use that message to give something to others at the same time?

—Alexandria Brown

Alexandria Brown is CEO of **Alexandria Brown International Inc.**, a multimillion dollar company devoted to empowering women around the world with the tools to living the freedom-based lives of their dreams via owning a successful business. Her marketing training products have helped thousands use email and the Internet to leverage their expertise, gain a broader reach, and dramatically increase their incomes. While Ali's best known for her expertise in marketing, her students share that her biggest impact comes from her philosophy of "designing your business to create an extraordinary life"™ — ensuring your business revolves around your own personal values and lifestyle. This, Ali says, is the most important key to bringing a business owner their ultimate wealth and happiness. You can learn more and subscribe to Ali's free articles at **www.AlexandriaBrown.com.**

CHAPTER

4

Dynamic Edge, Inc.

Developing a Culture of Giving

One of the best attributes of the City of Ann Arbor, Michigan, is its drive to make life better for the people living here. There are literally hundreds of non-profits in this city, working to provide services in just about any area you could imagine: from various health clinics to tutoring agencies, mentorship programs, museums, and even art galleries.

I started Dynamic Edge, Inc. while I was still in college with a backpack, a pair of size 10.5 rollerblades, and a decent-sized toolkit of computer skills that I had picked up over the years. We didn't have high-speed Internet, so we spent a lot of time in the computer labs doing research for our customers. It wasn't much, but it was enough to get started. There were a few clients at first. They were mostly friends and some small local businesses but with time, these people who I was helping with their computer problems began telling their friends about me.

So, from the very beginning, I knew that giving back to the community supporting my business was just as logical as it was ethical. Not only did I want to see philanthropy become a major component of the culture that Dynamic Edge was developing, I knew that it could broaden our reach into a community that is already very invested in the lives of its residents, and also that there were plenty of opportunities for us to get involved.

After the first 2 years of pounding the pavement to make things happen, Dynamic Edge started to take off. The business really began prospering when I took on a partner, Tim Neiman, who helped us transition from a fledgling operation into an organized (and rapidly growing) company. We moved from my small, off-campus apartment to a real-deal office that was big enough for all five of our employees to work. Things were coming together faster than I had really ever imagined. That was when we started thinking (learning, really) about things like mission and vision.

Knowing that in order to stay in business, we needed to make money, we taught our team to "make an honest profit delivering professional technology-related solutions."

There are plenty of other folks out there providing similar services, and we recognized that this would be the factor that made us stand out against the rest. The concept immediately resonated with both our staff and our clients. It was oblique enough that we could expand our services and, at the same time, it made clear that what we offered was computer-centered solutions.

It became our mission to see our clients thrive in a fluctuating business environment. So, by applying forward-thinking techniques and technology, we began to help prepare for the future. With the right people on our team, we knew that we could consistently provide a level of effort and care that not only surpassed our competitors, but also exceeded our clients' expectations.

It wasn't long before we realized that these values were helping us to establish strong, long-lasting relationships with our clients. Our staff was rapidly evolving into a fully functional team, and the camaraderie was almost magnetic. When our folks came in to work, they were glad to be there, and our clients became more like friends with almost every interaction. We all loved what we were doing — we were helping people solve problems and it felt really good.

The company's first charitable endeavor came from an unexpected source. We hadn't ever organized an actual fundraiser at that point, but a teacher friend of ours caught us off guard over drinks one evening.

She was talking about a program she had signed up to do with her classroom, but the grant she applied for wasn't enough to cover all of the supplies needed to implement the curriculum and they were considering pulling the plug. But, something in the story perked up our ears. It was the Palm Pilots. As a technology concierge, we see outdated equipment upgraded, recycled, or discarded almost every day. Immediately, we knew that this was an opportunity for us to help out a friend and her students.

Within two months, we had scrounged up enough gently-used Palm Pilots and reward credits through our partnership with Dell to fill in the gaps for the school program. Our small company had helped to put a Palm Pilot into the hands of every student in our friend's fourth grade class.

The day we made the presentation was a huge landmark for us as a team. We had our first taste of what it felt like to make a real difference in people's lives — people who weren't customers. In hindsight, there were a number of things we could have done differently to make an even bigger impact on that school. With the team we have now, we could have easily provided Palm Pilots for that school's entire fourth grade population, but the accomplishment itself wasn't nearly as important as its effect on our staff.

We've had a great time working with local non-profits during nearly 10 years as Dynamic Edge, and we've gotten to know some really great people in the process. I'd have to say that the relationships you develop working with people in your own community are probably the second greatest reward that comes along when you're helping other people. The first, obviously, is seeing how many people's lives are affected by a particular project. But it's that direct impact, really, that has set the criteria for our involvement in fundraising and charitable giving.

During our company's early years, our choice of projects and charities seemed almost arbitrary. Things would come up, we'd meet people who had a need, an idea would sound interesting, and we'd jump on board. It wasn't until a little bit later that we started seeking out opportunities where we could fill a void and really make a difference. Now, we regularly sponsor two charities through different events, and we have an ongoing Technology Grant Program.

One of our first major donations came through a team we put together to compete in the Detroit Free Press Marathon Relay. Spearheaded by Gordon Meyers (then one of our consultants and now one of our Team Leads) and Rebecca Lopez-Kriss (then the head of our marketing department), the Dynamic Edge Tech Trekkers banded together as a five-person running team that was enthusiastically committed to drumming up funds for Washtenaw Literacy, an organization dedicated to increasing community awareness about adult literacy.

Each year, Washtenaw Literacy helps more than 1,400 adults learn to read. They rely heavily on volunteer tutors and fundraisers to make ends meet. So, this idea was perfect for us. We had a group of people who really liked to run, and we knew we could get people to sponsor us for such a great cause. By accepting pledges for each of the 26.2 miles, we were able to bring in $1,700 to further the work of Washtenaw Literacy.

Our team completed the marathon in just over 4:12:00. Our team captain Gordon decided one week before the race that if our staff and his friends would pledge the first 25 miles, he would throw in the last 1.2 for free. He was so inspired at how much money everyone raised that he ended up doing the entire marathon instead of just his segment and finished the marathon in 4:25:43. Now, that's what I call dedication!

During the following year, we decided to do something to help folks during the holidays. As a kid, I remember waking up early one Christmas morning and driving our tractor up the road to visit some people my family knew from church. We drove the tractor because there was so much snow that particular morning that our car wouldn't get us through it, and my dad just kept saying that those kids needed to have presents on Christmas morning.

We were never wealthy, but my parents were always giving. They always gave, as they made it a priority in their life, and that was why I felt like we needed to do something during the holidays. So we organized Dynamic Edge's first ever canned foods drive. We did a little bit of searching and found a local group called Food Gatherers that affects nearly 6,000 people weekly by providing food and other items to needy families.

During the month of November, we ran a news flash on our website and talked to all of our customers about our plan, encouraging them to participate, and even offering to have their friendly Dynamic Edge consultant come to collect their donations on the last day of the drive. In just over one month, our staff and clients had pulled together 1,600 pounds of canned fish, stews, pastas, baby food, baking mixes, vegetables, peanut butter, and a good amount of personal care items!

The success of the Food Gatherers drive was so great that it created a ripple effect. We could see so much enthusiasm for giving that we knew we needed to do it again. The following year, we challenged one of our clients to a battle of the boxes and the stakes were high. When every item donated was accounted for and weighed, the team that lost the challenge had to serve lunch to the other team. Though Chelsea Rhone was a tough competitor, bringing in nearly 1,100 pounds, Dynamic Edge's determination brought in more than twice as much. The victory was sweet and lunch was delicious, but helping the Food Gatherers fill a truck with two-thirds of a ton of food and supplies was the biggest payoff of the competition. And we continue to collect for Food Gatherers every holiday season.

Aside from being great team-building opportunities, putting together a volunteer expedition or a fundraising effort allows everybody to work together on something other than computers. Our newest tradition of giving started last Thanksgiving through an event we called the "Christmas Beard Challenge." With Old Man Winter creeping up on us, we decided that we would all grow beards until Christmas and let our families, friends, and customers vote for their favorite for $1 a vote. As is usually the case, competition was tough with a majority of our staff participating, including Rebecca (although some have questioned the authenticity of her beard).

The big idea behind the beard competition was that more people would be able to participate and it was a longer lasting event than a marathon. The issue here is that we are computer people, and many of our people can't run that far. We're just way better at pushing buttons. We updated our website regularly to show the progression of the challenge, and pulled in a surprising 2,000 votes, which translated into another nice contribution to Washtenaw Literacy. We grew some pretty interesting beards and we're already working on a plan for this year's Christmas Beard Challenge, which will hopefully include time-lapsed photography of beard growth and real-time updates of votes tallied.

Because of our involvement in the marathon, the food drives, the beard contest, and Michigan Public Radio's Spring Fund Drive, we've spent a lot of time in the public eye. Doing things in the community has been great for business, but recently, it has reached the point where we're getting bombarded with requests for help. It became apparent to us that, in order to make the greatest impact that we can, we need to be donating along the lines of what our company does. That's why, in 2007, we established the Technology Grant Program.

When Ann Arbor's Pfizer plant closed, leaving a tremendous funding gap for area non-profits, we felt that small businesses in the area needed to step up to the challenge. We set up the Technology Grant Program to help local non-profit organizations fund a project they may have put aside due to funding issues, lack of expertise, or both. By using our time and resources, we have committed to assisting these organizations by kick-starting a specific IT project, by helping them assess and budget for long-term technology needs, or by assessing and maintaining an existing technology project.

In its current form, the program provides $7,500 annually to groups that can demonstrate a specific technology need, a substantial impact that the grant would make on the community through the organization and long-term sustainability.

During its first year, the Dynamic Edge Tech Grant program installed a Citrix Server for the National Kidney Foundation of Michigan, trained 826 Michigan's staff on how to use QuickBooks software to help keep the program and their records organized, and did a technology assessment and set up a long-term technology plan for the Hope Clinic of Ypsilanti. We completely redesigned the website for Special Days Camp and streamlined the public face of the organization. We also networked the computers at the Firehouse Museum and helped them set up a public computer work-station to access their library and archives.

As a company, Dynamic Edge has achieved consistent growth each year, and as the company continues to grow, I have a vision for enhancing the Technology Grant program as well. There are so many great organizations out there, just struggling to make ends meet, that could really benefit from the services Dynamic Edge has to offer through our grant program.

As a business owner, I am privileged to watch my employees embrace various causes and really dive into philanthropy. Two years ago, Jim Steinberger, a member of our team, decided that, because area schools aren't able to provide their students hands-on computer learning, he would start filling in the gap left by public school budget cuts. Creating his own unique curriculum and coordinating with students, teachers, parents, and the schools, Jim volunteered his own time to make sure that kids who shared his interest in technology would be able to access the training they needed. It was the least we could do to provide a learning space for them. So one night a week, the Dynamic Edge office, now located on State Street in a much bigger space, serves as a classroom for his 18 students. We also provided all of the technical equipment needed for the program.

I've realized in my years of running Dynamic Edge that, more than anything else, our company's culture is what sets us apart from our competitors — in our customers' eyes and our own. We make it a point to find the right people to join our team and then, giving them a chance to learn, lead, manage, and create in our work environment, we invite them get onboard with our philosophy of giving.

Every company has its own strategy and vision. While ours, understandably, involves becoming a growth engine in profit, we want to continue leading the competition as innovators of technology — to our customers, and also in our community. We have committed all of our skills and abilities to providing our communities with the same attention to detail as we do our customers, and I think that's what makes the biggest difference.

Giving back to your community in a real, tangible way is a feeling you don't easily forget. Once you've started doing things for the sake of doing good, it's really hard to stop. The same feeling we had presenting a small gift to one fourth grade classroom continues today in our staff of nearly 40. We continue to work in various ways throughout the community.

The "feel-good" factor is just one of several benefits for small businesses that support their communities. When you can use your business to accomplish great things and enable other organizations to succeed, it shows everybody how important it is to get involved, find a cause and help out. Other businesses will see what you are doing and get inspired. Anyone can start a chain reaction of positivity in the community. Philanthropy, when it is done right, can become contagious and rub off on business associations and even on your competitors, and everyone ends up benefiting from it.

—Bruce McCully

Bruce McCully is the founder of **Dynamic Edge, Inc.,** a company that helps take the guesswork out of computers for businesses of all sizes by providing the most comprehensive and effective technology solutions available. Offering custom programming, network installation and maintenance, web site development and hardware/software purchasing, we strive to bring businesses into a new age of profitability. Dynamic Edge's clients have access to a large, knowledgeable staff at a fraction of the cost of hiring one full-time IT professional… only we're on call 24 hours a day, 7 days a week.

Contact Information

Dynamic Edge, Inc.
2245 S. State Street
Ann Arbor, MI 48105
www.dynedge.com

CHAPTER

5

PearlParadise.com

Giving Back Campaign

I cannot remember how old I was, but I could not have been more than 8 or 9. I liked to read the newspaper with my grandparents and I saw a story that I thought was simply amazing. It was about a man who was very successful, rich by any standard, who was giving money away to people in need. He was not simply donating to charities and non-profit organizations, but actually accepting requests from individuals. People would write him a letter, explain their situation, and he would decide whether or not to help them.

I thought this man must have been an angel and wondered what it must feel like to have anything you wanted for yourself and still have enough money left over to help other people. It was nearly 30 years ago, but I can still remember reading that article with my grandmother.

About 11 years ago, I happened upon an unexpected opportunity. I was a flight attendant working for a major airline on layover in Beijing and some of my co-workers talked me into visiting the Hongqiao pearl market. I was not a shopper and had no interest in pearls at the time, but I went along anyway, somewhat grudgingly as I had intended to spend the day visiting the Great Wall.

At the pearl market I decided to buy a strand of pearls. They were cheap, I was there, and I did need to get my girlfriend a Christmas gift. I purchased a white strand of pearls for about $25. I had no idea whether they were worth the money I had paid, whether they were of good quality, or even whether my girlfriend would like the pearls.

I gave them to her a short time later and she loved them. She obviously thought they were much more valuable than I, as she decided to have them appraised. The jeweler who appraised them gave the strand a valuation of $600. The light bulbs went off. This was an opportunity.

Fast forward a decade and here I am today, the CEO of PearlParadise.com. We are the largest online pearl company in the world, with annual sales of nearly $25 million. We ship more than 250 pieces of finished pearl jewelry every day and have offices in five different countries. Making the early decision to market our product online has led to tremendous success beyond anything I could have hoped.

Giving back to the community was not something on my radar as I worked long hours over the years building this company. It was, however, something that my girlfriend (recipient of the first strand of pearls and now wife) became intimately involved in. She began working nearly as many hours as I did, but not making money. She volunteered her hours to animal rescue groups and any other charities that needed her help, financially or physically. I used to jokingly claim that we were responsible for spaying and neutering half the animal population of Los Angeles. Whenever there were fundraisers, we would always donate a piece of pearl jewelry for the silent auction. I became deeply involved as well, donating my time as well as financial assistance.

About a year ago, I found myself in an interesting position. As part of a business deal in China, I purchased a large lot of pearls that did not fit well into my company's product line. It was a package deal. I had to buy the lot in order to complete the transaction that was my real intention. But it meant that I had approximately 2000 strands of pearls that were incorrectly graduated in size, and we could not sell them without completely changing our product sizing structure. The strands of pearls sat in our vault for about a month before my wife had a brilliant idea. Why not give them away?

The strands of pearls we had given away in the past for fundraising auctions were very often the highlight of the night. They tended to raise quite a bit of money, much more than our actual cost. The retail value of a strand was approximately 1/10th the cost of the materials in China, and at fundraising auctions they routinely sold close to value.

In September 2007, we launched the Giving Back Campaign. We put out a press release, sent emails to all of our past customers, and contacted non-profits across the United States. Our message was simple. If any non-profits were having a fundraising event with a silent or live auction, we had a strand of fine quality pearls to give them. We created a special page on our website (**PearlParadise.com/giving**) with instructions on how to apply for a strand of pearls.

The response was immediate. Within the first month we were inundated with requests. The news spread quickly and soon we were shipping out dozens of packages each day. We had no choice but to assign one full-time associate specifically for this program. My wife assisted, of course. Nearly every type of non-profit imaginable applied for a strand of pearls. We sent every one of them a strand. We did not turn down a single application.

Soon we started receiving letters, thank-you cards, even gift baskets from appreciative groups. These strands of pearls which had cost us less than $100 each were being auctioned off for $200, $500, even up to $3000; and all the money was going to non-profit organizations.

We had not expected such a response. It was almost scary. I asked myself at the beginning whether or not we had made a mistake. As requests continued to pour in, it seemed as if it would never end. But we were generating so much in donations, more than we could have possibly hoped to give outright. We were making a huge difference in so many organizations.

There was quite a bit of cost involved, indeed. But there was a tremendous unseen benefit as well. Our sales began to increase dramatically. People would call and order pearls from us after seeing the donated strand of pearls at a benefit. The non-profits were putting our company name and logo on their own newsletters, on signs at the benefits, and in emails to their organization lists. Our Giving Back Campaign had become a source of income and a tremendous generator of good will.

In addition to the increase in sales the program generated, I also started to notice a strange shift in employee morale and attitude. In the beginning there was some company resistance to the idea of giving back to the national community, but it had become a company-wide effort, and now everyone was involved. We all began corresponding with different groups and learning about needs and issues that had been largely foreign to us. We really started to care. We could see the effects of our donations and the difference we were making in so many non-profits around the United States.

Below I have included something written by the associate in charge of the Giving Back Campaign. She expresses, in her own words, what the campaign has meant for her.

Anna Kerrigan:

After a year hiatus, I returned to work at PearlParadise.com looking for a project I could call my own. I was also looking for work that went beyond fashion sales to show a different side to pearls. Though pearls are a jewelry staple, they encompass much more. Pearls elicit an emotional response from people. I have witnessed this many times, from customers and my own family alike.

When I was asked to head the "Giving Back" program I was excited on many levels. I was happy to add something new to my work and welcomed the fresh outlet to connect with people and help. I also knew that my boss's wife was heavily involved in animal rescue. Doing something that was in line with the values of our president made me feel important and valued. I was eager to impress by devising a system that would ensure accuracy and raise money for large and small causes.

Jeremy's attitude makes the selection process a breeze. I send a $500 pearl necklace to every genuine organization. My one criterion for the donation is that the organization takes the time to fill out our application, or establishes some form of personal contact. This shows that they are interested enough to provide us with the information we were looking for.

When I prepare a shipment of donations I always email the participants and let them know that they have been accepted and should expect pearls to be arriving. Immediately after I send out an email, my inbox floods with "Thank You Anna!"s. The messages are usually short and immediate. It always impresses me how quickly these lovely emails arrive. I believe they reflect the genuine good will and hard work of the people behind the organization.

At first many of the organizations were animal-oriented. This was due to the personal contacts of Jeremy's wife with animal rescue. But quickly schools, health care organizations, and churches came pouring in. Once an auction was a success, I noticed that organizations from the same town would come in a bunch. Likewise, when a certain organization managed the promotions for an event, its subsequent events would come our way. I liked these trends, as they demonstrate the cooperative nature that charity work evokes.

On our website we posted a link to the "Giving Back Program." We also sent a email announcing the program to our customers. This link and email attracted some of our faithful customers to contact us personally to request a donation.

One of our most elaborate donations went to a woman who was organizing a gala for the Stray Cat Alliance in Beverly Hills. When she arrived at our office it was clear that she had style and dedication. She wore a pink sun hat and matching suit. Her hair was elegantly pinned back. She exuded old Hollywood. She was planning for everything to be pink, straight down to a special martini created solely for the gala. Her enthusiasm captivated our office. Because she was taking such care with detail, we decided to do something special for her event. After she left, Jeremy approached our jewelry designer and said, "Start designing a pearl cat collar." He then left to purchase the collars and we began feverishly brainstorming the many ways to combine pearls and cats.

Pearl Paradise is a busy office. It is rarely quiet and frequently punctuated by the immediacy of Jeremy's energy. Because it is also a very cooperative and friendly environment, when Jeremy has a problem with something, it is a big deal that everyone becomes privy to. In the beginning of the giving back process, Jeremy saw that one of the packages going out was in a snug-fitting priority mail envelope. He was seriously concerned. Director of Operations Mia Mesa met with me about this and offered to help. Mia and I agreed that from then on, we would pay the extra cost and send the donations via UPS in boxes.

The next day, Mia helped with the donation process. She was surprised by how involved and time-consuming it was. She ambitiously took ten donations to process, but after an hour, she completed only five. At that point, I believe she realized that "giving away" pearls sounded easier than it was in practice.

As time went on, the donation requests arrived faster and in larger groups. Subsequently, Christmas season began heating up and orders at

PearlParadise.com were more demanding. Jeremy quickly became concerned at the mammoth pile of donation requests bulging out of my "to be processed" folder. He came to me and said, "Let's just burn through them. We'll send them all out today!" In my head, I knew that although we had sent over 200 donations, there were still around 80 in my folder. I assured him we were not missing any events (I was sending them out by event date). Together Jeremy and I processed the remaining 80 donations and breathed a long sigh of relief. During this time, we both realized that accepting 80 requests for donations is easier than processing them. After this time, Jeremy would periodically peek into my office and ask me if I needed help. His vigilant concern added another level to my care and dedication to this work.

Jeremy also liked to know what number we were up to. I imagined that he used these little details as "pick-me-ups." How much we were contributing to worthy causes has been Pearl Paradise's immediate emotional boost at the end of a stressful day.

The following letter sums up the full fledged reach of giving back:

Dear Anna,

Thank you so much for your generous donation. It will make a wonderful item for our event. You have definitely found a customer for life and I will be referring you to all my friends and family — and now my school through this donation. Thank you so much for being great to work with and I look forward to ordering from you again in the future.

All the Best,
Alexis McGrath

Although the original Giving Back Campaign was only intended to continue until we had given away the 2000 strands of the "extra" pearls we had, this summer we decided to make the program permanent. We now purchase additional inventory with the specific intention of giving it away. We have also tailored the program to attract donation requests from groups that we most want to help.

In taking the Giving Back Campaign to the next level, we are now targeting specific groups while keeping the donations available to any and all groups that apply. Every quarter we have decided to select one genre of non-profit and send out a targeted press release along with an email campaign to individuals with ties to that segment of non-profits.

In August 2008, we decided to target animal rescue groups. We posted a press release online about our efforts to donate pearl strands to animal rescue groups around the United States. My wife also sent out an email "blast" to every rescuer in her address book — about 500 of them — with the request to forward the email to every animal rescuer they knew. Within a week we had already received hundreds of requests from around the United States. We received requests from rabbit rescues, dog rescues, horse rescues and even snake rescues. The message had gone viral.

I believe this program will be a permanent fixture in our company. It has opened our eyes so much to the world around us, and has given us another reason to come to work each day. We are making a difference to so many non-profit groups that exist for that very reason: to make a difference.

— **Jeremy Shepherd**, CEO, PearlParadise.com and **Anna Kerrigan**, Managing Director of Giving Back Campaign

Jeremy Shepherd is founder and CEO of **PearlParadise.com, Inc**. This relatively new company launched on the Internet in the late 1990's and quickly grew into the world's largest online seller of pearls, with annual sales exceeding $25 million.

Contact Information

10951 W Pico Blvd. Suite 100
Los Angeles, CA 90064
310-474-8788
www.PearlParadise.com

CHAPTER

6

Rick Steves' Europe Through the Back Door

Trinity Place: How and Why Rick Steves is Using his Retirement Nest Egg to House Homeless Mothers & their Children

The Roots of the Project

In my early travels — my "Europe through the gutter days" — my main challenge each day was finding a safe and affordable place to sleep. While traveling in Central America, I learned about how a rich country's policies (in this case, my country's) can cause landlessness (which means homelessness and hunger) in an underdeveloped country. This creation of a landless peasantry — at the mercy of an aggressive landowning class — reminded me of European feudalism. To think that the structural poverty that characterized those "dark ages" existed in our affluent and modern world was a shock to me. Then, after reading progressive books on hunger and homelessness (like Francis Moore Lappe's "Food First," Noam Chomsky's "Manufacturing Consent," and Arthur Simon's "Bread for the World"), I saw how structural poverty was an almost invisible but very real by-product of American capitalism, both within our country and abroad.

In about 1990, I had brainstorming sessions with my pastor on ways to house our local homeless. I came to believe that this is a real problem that the vast majority of people in our community choose not to see. To me, the problem had urgency and I wanted to do something about it. The next month, a ratty duplex adjacent to our church came up for sale. My wife,

Anne, and I had enough money to buy it ($80,000), and with the help of our church (Trinity Lutheran in Lynnwood) congregation to help maintain it, we offered it to Pathways for Women, a local non-profit that works with the YWCA to house local homeless moms and their kids.

Over the next decade, the duplex's three sisters on the same street went up for sale — each at an opportune time for us — and by the mid-1990s we had eight units in four duplexes in use housing homeless single mothers and their children. Eventually the buildings developed a mold problem and became uninhabitable. In 2002, we realized to ever have these buildings usable again; we'd need to invest lots of money in a clean up.

But to me, this was actually good mold. God was in that mold. We brainstormed — and the right move became clear. We'd tear down the duplexes and replace them with four-plexes, doubling the people we could house and creating a little community we'd call Trinity Way.

Trinity Way: A Pathways/YWCA/Rotary Club/Steves Collaboration

Until now this project was simply Anne and me offering the use of the duplexes to Pathways. This new vision was to solely finance 16 new units, deal with zone changes, plan thoughtfully, and oversee the construction. While we are providing the land and all the cash for the project (up to our $1 million ceiling for the four 4-plexes), our partners were providing substantial and essential services, without which, Trinity Way could never happen. The Rotary club joined in to motor the project to completion with their many talented members (architecture, project management, city relations, landscaping, furnishing, and so on). Anne and I would promise the free use of our buildings for 15 years. The Rotary Club would contribute various services as needed over the years. And Pathways/YWCA would manage the project with an obligation to the Steves to use the buildings to the absolute maximum capacity.

Defeated by Modern Building Codes

Our hope was to build Trinity Way for our $1 million budget. We demolished the old duplexes, hired an architect, contracted with a builder, and barreled ahead with our vision. Slowly it became clear, modern American building codes simply do not allow for basic utilitarian construction to provide safe and comfortable yet sparse temporary housing for homeless people. The buildings, the land . . . even the sidewalks needed "contour" so they would look nice. Landscaping requirements chipped away at play zones. Financial setback after setback drove the price up until a $200,000 drainage requirement drove the building price to $1.6 million — well beyond our combined budgets — and finally sealed the fate of the project. It was no longer a wise use of our limited capital.

A New Direction: Renovate an Existing Apartment "Trinity Place"

Rather than invest $1.6 million plus the land for 16 new units, we decided to look for existing apartment buildings (which would enable us to buy into the standards of an age with simpler codes). Trinity Way became Trinity Place. We located a 24-unit complex for the same amount of money (and that came with land to boot). Back on track, our vision — born in El Salvador, and matured with a long march through church meetings, mold, and suburban Seattle zoning codes — was finally within reach.

The location of Trinity Place couldn't be handier for people in transition (good access to public transit, groceries, Edmonds Community College, church). Purchasing the apartment in April, 2005, our partners (Pathways, the YWCA, and the Rotary Club) renovated the units and we're housing single mothers and their children by Thanksgiving, 2005.

Why Homelessness? Why Pathways?

As a man (in a male-dominated world), I take partial responsibility for the plight of women abandoned by their husbands to raise children alone. Pathways (which joined forces with the YWCA a few years ago) works very effectively in my community with exactly that problem as its focus. For me, Pathways/YWCA is not a charity. It's a service. I pay them to translate my excess productivity into fighting this problem. Since I've already consumed all I really need, this gives me the treat of vicarious consumption. It's a fun way to consume beyond my capacity.

Single moms have so many cards stacked against them and society almost seems to blame them. I have an affinity for these women because I have friends and relatives who have been in this overwhelming and very discouraging me-and-my-kids-against-the-world situation.

I think the issue of homelessness strikes a chord with me, in part, because of my travels. For years, as a teenage vagabond slumming around Europe not knowing where'd I'd sleep tonight — sleeping in train stations, or sacked-out, frightened, in city parks — allows me to relate to being cold, wet and lonely through the night. While this was a perspective-altering experience, I had no kids to care for and a plane ticket home. I can't imagine the weight of having no money, no roof over my head, no job, and small children to care for.

Mixing Motivations: as a Christian and as a Businessman

As a businessman, I feel it's a responsibility to make a real commitment to my community. And, it's my hope that a project like this — utilizing a local agency like Pathways/YWCA as a service more than a charity — will inspire business people to think creatively about making a real difference this way. In a time with greater human need and lesser return on conventional investments, simply redefining "returns" suddenly makes this a smart use of capital.

As a Christian, I believe in tithing. And as a Christian businessman, I think a business can have this kind of giving as a goal too. A business has a lot of potential for good in its community. In my creative charitable initiatives, I hope to inspire other business people to do more than canned food drives. I was inspired this way back in the early 1980s when I met with a group of local business people who were supporters of Seattle's World Concern (a relief agency working for caring Seattleites in the developing world). I hope Trinity Place inspires other individuals, businesses, and charitable organizations to creatively use their capital (even if on a smaller scale) to buy simple existing housing to equip non-profits to help our homeless.

We Can Make a Choice: A Thousand Points of Light or an Enlightened Society

As an American and a liberal, I'm tired of hearing people say "there's not enough money." With any honest assessment, there is enough money. In fact, there is more money than ever. But we as a society have different priorities. As a Democrat, I believe providing affordable housing (like health care and education) is a responsibility of society in general — implemented efficiently by government. But I'm willing for now to be proceeding in the "thousand points of light" and "faith-based" Republican style which prefers to let the people who really care handle the problem apart from government involvement. But I do this under protest. I believe this can and should be performed most fairly and efficiently with governmental initiative by society as a whole. In short, an enlightened society brightens its world in unison and doesn't need a thousand points of light.

A Political Backdrop . . . Driven by "Class Warfare"

I believe our current government is motivated primarily by the greed of its corporate and wealthy patrons. President Bush's passions need to be understood in economic terms — how each initiative enriches the groups whose financial support put him and his party in power. Military expenses (about 50 percent of our governments discretionary budget and as much as the rest of the world combined) enriches Americans who make and sell arms. Privatization of social security pumps more money into Wall Street. Prescription benefits drives up the deficit (which future tax payers will have to pay) in order to enrich the pharmaceuticals. Our "war on terror" allows us to secure oil and gas interests in West Asia and the Middle East. ("Freedom" for Afghanistan means huge new military bases protecting a vital new gas pipeline through that country — which almost no one sees as taxpayer-subsidized corporate welfare.) Tax cuts for the wealthy and various forms of corporate welfare make it urgent that we squeeze "discretionary domestic" budget items (which is a kind of warfare on the poor both in America and abroad). All the domestic squeezing in the name of fiscal discipline saves around $60 billion. This is a paltry number compared to the hidden windfall each category above brings to corporations and the wealthy. The last thing a wealthy person like me needs is a huge tax cut. You'd be surprised (and probably outraged) if you know how much money I have saved as President Bush has cut my taxes in order to squeeze our poor and inflate our deficit.

Global Needs Trumped by Local Homelessness

For me proximity has nothing to do with suffering and need. I believe that if $1,000 helps more people in a distant land than here in the USA, investing it abroad is better stewardship of that charitable resource. That can be a tough sell in America. And many believe in "keeping it local" and helping the person across the street rather than across the ocean. You can't jam a world perspective into the minds of people who have not traveled. And people who've not traveled are often actually put off by a global concern that has no local concern element to it.

In investing my retirement funds in Trinity Place, I know that same money could help more people in a developing nation. While over the last 20 years I've enjoyed many creative charitable ventures for hungry and homeless people oversees, now my wife and I want to balance that with this local initiative. After Trinity Place is up and running, we can focus vigorously on more distant concerns knowing that we're balanced with a strong and local project. I hope this will help people be more open to my global perspective on human needs.

The Financial Arrangement Between the Steves and Pathways/YWCA

The Steves provide and own the apartment complex. Pathways and the Rotary club see that the units are renovated and fit to house clients of Pathways/YWCA. Pathways/YWCA will manage the project in a way where the Steves have no risk, no expense, and no income for 15 years. During this time, Pathways will charge a small rent to its clients who stay in Trinity Place in order to have a budget covering taxes, insurance, utilities, and general maintenance. The Steves own the buildings and have the option to take them back for their own non-charitable use after 15 years, with one-year notice. In 15 years, we turn 65 and will have access to the buildings for our retirement if we choose.

Are you not just Enabling People to Live off Charity?

The "give a man a fish and he's fed for a day or give him a net and teach him to fish and he's fed for a lifetime" thinking is pure wisdom to Anne and me. So when we support something, we want to do it in a way that empowers people to become self-sufficient. Providing a resource for Pathways for Women/YWCA to house homeless moms and their kids empowers Pathways to do the important work they are so good at: helping these single mothers get back on track and build lives in which they can raise their children with dignity. I meet people routinely here in Edmonds who came upon tough times, were supported by Pathways, and are now happy and well-settled members of our community again. I wish these success stories made headlines.

Smart Investing — From "Europe on $5 a day" to "Dignity on $3 a day."

From a practical point of view, this "investment" is ideal for anyone who can enjoy the "vicarious" consumption of a homeless person getting a safe and comfortable place to sleep. Think of our rewards. Put a $1.4 million in a CD and you earn maybe $80,000 in taxable interest (which would be about $50,000 after taxes). With this investment, our taxable income is zero. But we know that we are providing 24 moms and probably 46 children a home. That's housing for about 70 people at a cost to us of $800 a year (less than $3 a day) each. In my work of finding budget travel places to eat and sleep, this is a real turn-on. So, that's my selfish little pleasure: I stow my money in a safe place and as a return, rather than taxable income, Anne and I know we're housing all these people. What would we do consuming an extra $50,000 a year? How much joy would that car, condo at Whistler, yacht, or whatever bring us? About one percent of the joy we get from helping 70 people (indirectly through the work of Pathways/YWCA). That's our kind of investment.

The same can be done on a smaller scale. An affordable housing investor could invest $200,000 in a simple duplex; let their church or local homeless organization use the property. Rather than $14,000 in taxable interest (about $9,000 after tax annually), you're housing two families — six people. Real people being housed by you for $1,500 a year or $5 a day each . . . what a wonderful kind of passive income.

And, by partnering with hard working charities whose passions are the same as yours, you don't need a million dollars to get these royal returns. This isn't altruism, it's just common sense and compassion.

—Rick Steves

Rick Steves (**www.ricksteves.com**) writes European travel guidebooks and hosts travel shows on public television and public radio. E-mail him at **rick@ricksteves.com**, or write to him c/o P.O. Box 2009, Edmonds, WA 98020.

CHAPTER

7

Beauregard Stubbs

An Artist's Way of Making a Difference

Beauregard Stubbs was created in 2004 as a company for dog lovers. Not just another company for dogs *per se,* but for those of us with large breed dogs who wanted their loved dogs to also have choices that were fashionable beyond the nylon collar and leash! We began by featuring retro-style accessories, made with one-of-a-kind, vintage fabric as well as soulful yet whimsical custom pet portraits. I'm getting a bit ahead of myself — let me fill you in on our history.

As a recent graduate of Pasadena Art Center College of Design, I was taking on all kinds of different creative products. At that time I was working on a wedding invitation for a couple with a beautiful Bull Terrier, Stella, who ended up being the first, official pet portrait. The painting of Stella was an engagement gift for the bride-to-be. Stella was so thrilled with her mirror image that she ended up sealing every invitation that was sent out! And this inspiration is how Beauregard Stubbs was born.

It more than conveniently combined two of my passions: my art and my love for canines. Having had two Basset Hounds of my own, I was forced to face the very difficult task of having to choose between the two little muses — Daisy OR Lucy? I decided to name the company after my mom's childhood Basset Hound, Beauregard, and combined my two girls into one persona for the portrait that would become the iconic image and logo for this small and enthusiastic company.

My business partner in all this was my soon-to-be sister in law, Julie Klingsberg. We worked well together and enjoyed each other's company, making plenty of mistakes and drawing lots of excitement and inspiration from late nights with Lyle Lovett playing in the background. These nights and endless hours of design are what formed Beauregard Stubbs' first product line. Our motto was "Dogs aren't our whole life, but they make our lives whole," a quote from Roger Caras which perfectly described how we felt. Julie spent time designing and sewing bags, backpacks, puppy pads, and doggy poopy pouches with a vintage flair, seeking constant feedback from my design background and experienced eyes. During this time I spent my time painting to my heart's content. I came up with more and more designs and increased my skill with each painting, attempting to capture each dog's personality through paint and canvas.

In the midst of all this Julie started a doggie boarding and daycare out of her home to help fund the vintage fabrics, buttons, ribbons, fringes, and bows. I continued to paint, each time getting a little closer to capturing the true persona of each dog I painted. People have commented that if you review my work, you can find the dog's soul in their eyes within my paintings.

During this time we opened a small boutique in Fallbrook that combined the inspiration of Beauregard Stubbs and saving dogs . . . so I got to go back to the drawing board and created a logo for our vintage, dog-friendly boutique — Bones & Scones! I hand-painted the sign and it is still a reminder of our earliest days together.

At our store we featured an adoptable dog of the week for the customers to visit as well as learn about the plight of homeless dogs. We featured our line of products along with vintage figurines of dogs of course. Our first regular dog of the week was a Great Dane named Kane, a six-year-old, grey muzzled Dane who was taken to the local veterinary office to be put to sleep. Why? you might ask. Well, Kane's owner put in new wood floors (this story comes full circle so hang tight . . .). We would hold regular adoption events at the store, fun fundraising days in which I would create photo cards and we'd pull out the old Polaroid and snap shots of friendly visitors who took along a gift of a photo of their dog, neat and tidy in a Beauregard Stubbs memorable gift card. The proceeds went straight back into our dog rescue efforts, one at a time.

As the Klingsberg Doggy Ranch got more and more of a regular client base, Julie's schedule got a bit crazier; with three kids and who knows how many dogs each day, her time to work on our project together became more and more scarce. Her brother, Mark Allen Miller, who I had met years ago, but reunited with at Art Center, popped the inevitable question and slapped a ring on my finger. The wedding plans became the central focus of my days, time, and enthusiasm. My soon-to-be husband and I, both being artists, did the entire wedding ourselves, from the invitations to the table settings. His eye for color and gift for designing flowers and my art skills made a wedding that was not only beautiful but also personal because it was all ours; design, concept and us — a truly beautiful union.

Life happens while you are making plans, and Beauregard Stubbs took a hiatus from the public eye.

When the wedding bells had finally chimed, Julie's little doggy day care had become a full-fledged, incorporated, non-profit public charity functioning as an all-breed, all-age, all-size dog rescue. Critter Crossings was up and running. She was out saving dogs from death row in our local shelters full-time and Beauregard Stubbs was now completely back in my hands.

You may be thinking this is the end of this story, but in all honesty, this is only the beginning!

After getting married and having moved away from my sweet little Daisy and Lucy (mom insisted they stay with her and at the ripe old age of 12 and 13 I had to reluctantly agree) life took some turns and got interesting.

Julie's rescue saved a litter of abused, abandoned, beaten, and starved purebred Boxer puppies. Having seen the photos of their condition, we could not stop ourselves from stepping up to help our sister. After fostering one of the babies to help out the rescue and separate this litter to give them the best chance at life, we found ourselves in love and Banjo Marie became our first fur child.

Her siblings all had broken bones, brain trauma, behavior concerns, you name it, and they had been through the worst as pups. Banjo's parents found a purebred rescue as well. Our baby was skin and bones when we got her, but so thankful for the smallest touch and the constant meals, she gave us back nothing but kisses and wiggles. It was Banjo who really changed the direction of Beauregard Stubbs. It was impossible to believe anyone could hurt something this tiny, fragile, and preciously cute. It is daunting to become awakened and exposed to animal abuse and neglect. Sadly, once enlightened, you can never turn back — only move forward to save more.

And the way I chose to contribute to saving more dogs like Banjo was through my gifts, talents, and studies. I worked harder than ever creating portraits to donate to animal rescue charity auctions; sometimes raising funds for a specific dog in need, like another Boxer, damaged beyond a suitable description here. This dog did not deserve her fate — she lived, yes, but lost her leg after a month in the hospital and $6000 in veterinary charges. I had to think of something. I had to figure out a way for people to easily donate and give them something creative back. The solution? Go digital. With Valentine's Day right around the corner, "Hearts for Hurley" was created. A valentine that could be customized for each and every donor who sent in five dollars. Why FIVE DOLLARS you ask? Because five times a thousand and well, we saved her life that's all. At this point our motto switched to the age-old saying, "Saving just one dog won't change the world, but surely the world will change for that one dog!"

Our little Banjo was growing into quite the active dog. We nicknamed her the deer and she was constantly making us laugh with her figure eights around the backyard. Then came the limp. A veterinary consult determined that she was born with hip dysplasia as a result of backyard breeding. We came up with a solution to invest $4,000 in the near future to replace her hips or search for a mature dog to settle Banjo down. On my way back from this vet visit, I happened to be picking up a dog to take down to the rescue group in San Diego. Distracted and distraught over Banjo's prognosis, I honored my commitment and picked up this sweet, very scared girl.

Gigi looked like a giant, 70-pound Boston terrier. Banjo was trying to play with her the entire drive home, and tolerant Gigi just rolled with the punches. We dropped Banjo off at home, for her doctor ordered crate rest (three miserable weeks) and continued on to Julie's house. Poor Gigi was completely lost; the dogs, the kids, too many new faces to not be overwhelmed. She stayed glued to my side, and although I hated having to turn right around and leave her, I had to get back to my ailing Banjo. After much deliberation, Julie convinced me to come back a week later for Gigi. She hadn't bonded to anyone at the Klingsberg house, her stress levels increased each day, and didn't the doctor order a calm girl for Banjo?

We decided to give our first time at fostering a shot and brought Gigi home. There was one major obstacle. Gigi had been beaten by a man and cowered whenever Mark got near. Banjo and Gigi, on the other hand, were a match. She was Banjo's perfect alpha dog counterpart. It took months for Gigi to trust Mark, yet she slowly grew to love him. Our little family added a member and Gigi gained her middle name. Gigi Louise just made my commitment to help these dogs even stronger. How many more dogs like Gigi were out there just needing a chance to learn to trust again?

My dedication became stronger as the messages became even more apparent to me. It is amazing how ignorant I was in the past. I have been fortunate to affiliate with my sister's group in its earliest days and have met many dogs, leading to more and more inspirational work. I am personally responsible for rescuing over 40 dogs, and I have been the person to face the front lines in the shelter, having to leave with only one, maybe two, dogs, seeing faces behind bars that are wondering if anyone will come for them.

I take the opportunity of visiting the shelters to use my professional photography skills and capture the desperation of the dogs that find themselves abandoned and alone. Once home and all cried out I get artistic with these images. I add clever yet pointed messages to their photos. The messages represent the causes I fight for and believe in — spaying and neutering, the plight of senior dogs, purebred dogs, and dogs that need just the investment of medical attention in our local shelter. All have been left there, alone and scared. The least I can do is take their photos and make people aware that not all shelters are filled with "bad," "dumb," or "aggressive" dogs.

Along with the photography, I kept designing digitally, getting my designs out in any way I could to support my beliefs. My designs can be found throughout many MySpace pages, on t-shirts, on many websites, and used as profile images for the latest cause I am supporting. They have a distinctly familiar look to people because, you see, I donate most of my free time to animal rescue and getting the message out in a friendly, easy-to-digest way. If something is well designed it attracts more people. Who doesn't want to wear a cute shirt? And if the money spent on it goes back to saving dogs, well, it doesn't get much better than that!

Remember Kane? Here is where it comes full circle. One very cold rainy day in January, I got a frantic call from Julie. "Kane, Kane is in Temecula," she screams over the phone. It was Kane, Critter Crossings' very first rescue dog, the beautiful purebred brindle Great Dane.

A good Samaritan who happened to be familiar with rescued dogs through their grooming business found Kane running through traffic. He had no tags and no collar, but thankfully, his microchip remained registered to the rescue group. I drove to pick him up, anticipating a very old feeble guy because at this point he was 10 years old. Then, there he was, the same sweet boy. Happy, active, with just a little more grey on the muzzle, which is an estimate of beauty in my mind, and a bit underweight. He came into our house a bit skittish and reserved; not quite sure what to think about my other two rescue babies Banjo, a rambunctious Boxer pup, and Gigi, an easy-going alpha girl, an Olde English Bulldogge.

Slowly, he worked his way into my pack, put on some much-needed weight, and continued to steal everyone's heart that had the chance to be in his presence. It was at that point I knew it; I was a foster failure. There was no way this sweet old guy was going to have to go to a new home again, ever. So then there were three, Kane Herman finished our pack. Today, I am the person who has adopted three neglected, abused, and abandoned dogs. Even though all I've ever really wanted is a French bulldog, with proper education, the idea of spending a couple grand on one puppy is just not an option. There are just too many lives that need to be saved.

With Kane my love for Great Danes grew, and as usual, a new art project began. I had been doing so much digital work and really missed getting my hands dirty. I wanted to find a way to do breed-specific art, get back to the vintage feel Beauregard had started with, and make something a little more accessible to the public. I kept coming back to silhouettes. I had always loved them but wanted to find away to reinvent them. So, I started cutting the canines out of vintage patterned paper. I was inspired! Fun multi-colored canvases covered my walls, featuring all my favorite breeds. I debuted them by donating one to a Boxer in need and the response was overwhelming. More breed enthusiasts requested their dogs be represented. I accommodated their requests, and quickly doubled the breeds represented.

Beauregard Stubbs' website is consistently changing and expanding. Along with a store, a blog has been started not only to let people know Beauregard news, but also to feature adoptable dogs, adoption events, and any news on the dogs who have already been featured. Of course, there are always plenty of pictures of my happy dog pack!

Once you know, you really know what happens to all of the animals that society chooses to abandon, you cannot turn a blind eye. At least I cannot. So I choose to use my gifts, my talents, my artful eye, and my skills to help promote, raise funds, network, and creatively help those who help others in need. My work has always been my passion and now my passion has expanded into being able to do both daily, which in my opinion, is a gift in and of itself.

—Karen Halker

Karen Halker is Proprietor and Artist for **Beauregard Stubbs.** We are a tiny company with a big heart. Our products are made especially for dog lovers, and devoted to giving the underdog a second chance. We feature custom portraits, along with vintage style paintings.

Contact Information

www.beauregardstubbs.com
Seal Beach, California

CHAPTER

8

French Mortuary & the French Family of Companies

A Legacy of Giving

In 1904, my grandfather, Chester T. French, was teaching in a one-room schoolhouse when he learned that his younger brother had tuberculosis. At that time, the best treatment for tuberculosis was to live in a dry climate. Wanting the best treatment for his brother, he determined that the city with the most promise for his brother's recovery and the possibility of work for him was Albuquerque, New Mexico.

They made the long train trip from their home six miles south of Knoxville, Tennessee. When they arrived in Albuquerque they lived in a tent due to limited resources. Unfortunately, it wasn't long after they arrived that my grandfather's younger brother's health completely failed him and he died. The process of planning to get his brother back home to Knoxville, Tennessee had a powerful impact on him. Over the course of the train trip back to Tennessee, he reconsidered his original desire to become a Methodist minister. He told me that after reflecting on the painful grieving process he was going through while assuring that his brother had a respectful service and burial, he was struck by the loneliness of the process. At that moment, he recalled that he began sensing a call to become a funeral director — he saw funeral service as an opportunity to minister to people in their greatest time of need.

In 1907, Mr. French, or "Papa French" as those of us around him called him, opened French Mortuary with a desire to not only serve and minister to families, but to make a difference in the community by contributing his time, his talent, and his treasures. Over the years, he served in leadership positions in many organizations, including his church, County Commission, Community Chest (now United Way), Kiwanis, and YMCA, to name only a few. He had a great love for young people and founded the Chester T. French Boy's Choir (now called the Albuquerque Boy Choir). Along with his wonderful friends, Lloyd and Wanda Higgins, he helped start Hummingbird Music Camp, located in the Jemez Mountains near Albuquerque, which, 50 years after its founding, continues to musically train hundreds of young people each summer under the direction of the Higgins family. He also taught a Sunday school class for more than 40 years, and he provided dozens of scholarships to the University of New Mexico. Since his philanthropy was so well known, in 1965, McMurray College honored him with a Doctor of Letters degree.

In 1964, at the age of 82, Mr. French asked me, his grandson, Chester French Stewart, to work with him in the mortuary business. Later, I was joined by my two younger brothers Bob and Rick, both of whom remain very active in the business, as does my son, Bill, who began working with us after attending college. At the age of 84, Mr. French, the founder of French Mortuary, civic leader, and beloved grandfather, died. He had served as CEO of French Mortuary for 59 years. I served the company in that capacity for 41 years from 1966 to 2007 — which means that in our first 100 years our company had only two CEO's. Now, I remain Chairman of French Mortuary and the French Family of Companies but, effective January 1, 2008, relinquished the title of President/CEO.

In the year prior to my grandfather's death I was listening as he talked to a man who had come in to the mortuary to ask him for some financial help. He took a personal interest in the man, asking him about his life and his family. He did provide some financial help for him. A little later, while we were driving in the car together, I told him that I had been listening to the conversation and I felt the man had perhaps taken advantage of him. I have never forgotten his reply. "If he took advantage of me that is his problem because I did what I thought was right."

Several months after Mr. French's death, a young man came to see me bringing a gift, and he recounted this story, "When my son died as an infant while my wife was still in the hospital, I had no idea how I would find the resources to have a proper service. Someone at the time suggested I go see Mr. French, describing him as a very kind man who was very sensitive to the needs of the community. I did just that. I went to French Mortuary that afternoon to see him. Your grandfather was so loving and kind to me. He put his hand on my shoulder and said, "Young man, you don't need to worry, we are going to take care of your baby." And he did, at no expense to me. My family and I will never forget this act of kindness."

Two years later, because of this experience, we made a company decision that we would provide funeral services at no cost to families who experience the death of an infant. We believe that this is another way we can minister to families who are grieving upon the death of a baby, and are often struggling financially, as well. We see this as an important and meaningful way that we can give back to our community.

In the years that followed, French Mortuary has continued to grow, and today it is one of the largest family-owned funeral service establishments in the country. During my 41 years as both Chairman and President/CEO, I have continued to the fullest of my ability to follow the model set by my grandfather — often tough shoes to fill. I have been actively involved in my church, Rotary, the Better Business Bureau, the New Mexico Holocaust Museum, and Noon Day Ministries, just to mention a few. Mr. French often said, "If you live in a community, you must give back."

Generosity is more than simply writing a check and dropping it in the mail. Our society today is so absorbed by "getting the most toys" that it's easy to miss what truly brings real blessings and joy, the genuine inspiration found through working with and helping others. The Lord himself said, "It is more blessed to give than to receive." That simple notion — that we're empowered and that we can know true joy by reaching out to help others — has served as a central guide for my work, as well as the work of our company. In addition to receiving and reviewing requests from organizations that seek to partner with us on community projects, we actively pursue opportunities to help non-profits who can contribute to our charitable giving goals. In 2007, we contributed over $240,000 in addition to substantial personal gifts. Halfway through 2008, we have already contributed to more than 65 local organizations representing health services, education, community support, and the arts.

The people of the French Family of Companies are some of the most compassionate people you can ever hope to meet. Because of their generosity, we offer to match dollar for dollar all contributions our employees make up to $250 for everyone on staff. Additionally, our leadership team's personal contributions are matched up to $1,000 when giving to one of our focused giving areas: the arts, education, community services, and senior services. Our volunteer projects echo these gifts and strive for results that are important to the community and our employees. Everyone on staff at French Mortuary and our family of companies is encouraged to give as their hearts lead them and to serve as leaders in the non-profit community. We endeavor to help staff find organizations that will provide them with ample opportunity to use their unique talents to serve our community. As a result, our staff is active in over 80 community organizations.

To help meet our quarterly giving goals, the entire company participates in community service projects. In the past these have included collecting and distributing school supplies, collecting food for the Albuquerque Rescue Mission, putting together Christmas and Thanksgiving care packages, and many walk-a-thons and golf tournaments benefiting many of our local charity organizations. Because French continues to be a family-owned business, we are keenly aware of our community's needs, and we endeavor to respond quickly to meet them and to celebrate our participation.

The Lord talked about money and possession in at least one-third of his parables. Matthew 6:29 says, "Where your treasure is, there your heart will be also." It is much easier to give to the things we love. We really do believe that our gifts can make a difference for eternity. Earthly treasures simply do not last. Psalms 49:16 & 17 says, "Do not be overawed when a man grows rich, when the splendor of his house increases; for he will take nothing with him when he dies, his splendor will not descend with him." We cannot take it with us but we can send it on ahead.

We are committed to giving back to our community. For example, through the United Way of America and the de Tocqueville Society in 2007, the president of the company, Donald F. "Duffy" Swan, and I jointly co-chaired the city's 2007 fundraising campaign. The 2007 campaign was recognized by the National Alexis de Tocqueville Society for its excellence. Receiving five of a possible nine national de Tocqueville awards, the campaign added a record 80 new members, bringing the number of givers of $10,000-or-more members to an amazing 426, a remarkable achievement for a medium sized community. This helped the United Way of Central New Mexico to be #1 in per capita giving in the country. But what truly made the difference for the two of us was the sheer joy of helping others see the pleasure in giving and knowing all the good the contributions would make in our community. It was an opportunity to use our influence to make our city and state a much better place.

On November 7, 2007, we celebrated French Mortuary's 100th Anniversary. To mark the company's 100-year history of supporting our community, we decided to give back in ways we had never done before. We contributed $100,000 over and above our established philanthropic budget, designating gifts in four areas in our community: the arts, economic development, healthcare, and community services. 2007 was a remarkable year in many ways. We received the Outstanding Business/Corporation in Philanthropy Award from the New Mexico Chapter of the Association of Fundraising Professionals for our commitment to making a difference in the community. It's hard to take credit for something you know should be done and that we would have done anyway, but we were honored and sincerely desire to set a positive example for other companies to follow. Six years earlier French Mortuary received the Ethics in Business Award, from the Good Samaritan Counseling Center, the only funeral service company in the state to be honored. We believe our philanthropy is an important part of ethics.

Prior to joining the French Family of Companies in 2004, Duffy Swan had a long history of philanthropy, including service as the University of New Mexico's Director of Development and President of its Foundation. Duffy is a past recipient of the New Mexico Ethics in Business Award as well as the New Mexico Philanthropy Award. All of these things, as you can imagine, made him the ideal candidate to assume the role of CEO of French Mortuary and the French Family Companies on January 1, 2008 — only the third CEO in our company history. I knew that Duffy would carry the same vision and the same commitment to give back that we have held for over 100 years.

In keeping with tradition and Mr. French's mission, the French Family of Companies will continue adding to our long history of serving and giving back to the community, aspiring with each contribution to connect with the community and make a difference. The Lord gives us each the opportunity to experience true joy, by reminding us that "it is more blessed to give than to receive." We are committed to continue sharing with our community, knowing that we will continue to be blessed. It is the goal of French Mortuary and the French Family of Companies to continue to be an example of joyful giving, knowing that "where our treasure is there will our hearts be also."

— **Chester French Stewart,** Chairman, French Mortuary & The French Family of Companies

French Funeral Services is New Mexico's largest and oldest family-owned funeral service company, founded by Chester T. French in 1907. The tradition of caring for New Mexico families began at Fifth Street and Gold Avenue in old downtown Albuquerque. French Funeral Service has grown over the last 100 years and now serves families through four funeral service locations, Sunset Memorial Park cemetery and mausoleum, Best Friends pet cremation services, Albuquerque Monument and Engraving memorial services, and Heritage advance planning services.

CHAPTER

9

Eleven Limited, LLC

Give More Than You Take

Since my earliest days I was taught that family, a strong work ethic, and giving back to the community were the three pillars upon which one could build a robust sense of satisfaction and success in life.

My dad was always a hard worker. While we were growing up, he often worked two or three jobs and we rarely saw him for long periods of time. Sundays were the exception; he would make time for "Family Day" and take my brother, sisters, and me to a special event, a museum, or just out to get ice cream. To him hard work was just one of the things you did to provide for your family. As a child I never really understood the importance of what he was doing. But as I grew to manhood, I began to see the importance of the commitment he had made to us, to his work, and to his community.

My mother also gave a great deal to her community. And it is from her, perhaps, that I received my fiercely independent and entrepreneurial spirit. Mom had always been an avid gardener. I don't mean the type of gardener who goes out into her garden once a week to cut flowers for the kitchen table. She was the kind of gardener who would work the earth day in and day out, seven days a week from dusk till dawn until her bones ached. When we were younger, she started what we call the Daze End Herb Farm. On this farm, we learned to work the soil with our hands, to plant the earth using our heads and with our hearts — to see the beauty of our work.

As I grew older, and my thoughts began to mature, I began to understand the lessons my parents had been teaching me all along through their thoughts and through their deeds. What they had really been teaching me and my siblings is that we should — we must — give more than we take.

So you see, giving to the community, even at the expense of my own personal time and money, is something I believe is embedded in my own DNA. It's not something I can really control; it's something that must be done. Something I simply have to do.

Genesis

Eleven Limited is not the first small business I have started, it is simply the latest iteration in what I believe to be a continuum of works that benefit my family while simultaneously giving back to the community. But to me, Eleven Limited seems different than the other companies I started. As soon as it was off the ground I realized this would be a wonderful opportunity for me to make some money for myself and my family while at the same time finding a way to give back to the community in terms of both services and money. It may seem odd perhaps that these thoughts would occur to an entrepreneur simultaneously. But to me, they just seemed natural.

Giving — from the very start

Charitable giving started from the very beginning with Eleven Limited. I realized that there were many small businesses out there that would not be able to afford the costs involved with full-blown web development, web and graphic design, and web hosting. With that in mind, I decided that if I got a solid handle on my costs and set my profit margin at a reasonable level, I would be able to charge people less than they might find on the open market. With this as a base, I realized I could generate a solid customer foundation using this pricing model and insure a positive cash flow. With this structure I would be able to search out various areas where I felt that I could support the community either through financial donations or through my web development skills.

Looking for a model of success

When asked to write this chapter of the book, I decided to look back at my experiences to see if there were any role models I had based my giving upon: I drew a blank. In the beginning I was keenly focused on growing the company and that growth simply included a giving component.

In college when we were looking at various business models and applying Maslow's hierarchy of needs to corporate structures, corporate giving always ended up at the very apex of the hierarchy of needs only after the company had made enough money and was secure in its standing in the marketplace.

My model stood that hierarchy on its head. My thinking was such that if I were to structure this business properly, then I wouldn't need to wait until we had amassed great amounts of wealth or large market share. We could begin charitable giving immediately.

The societal need as seen through the eyes of one business owner

I would say giving is critical to the success of my business because I truly believe that if we want to make a change in our communities we can't wait for someone else to do it for us. We need to be the change in our communities. We are not entities that are acted upon by random factors in the universe, I believe that we actually create our own destinies, and we are responsible for those destinies. If we want to live in a better place, a place where people care about their neighbors, where they care about their communities, and where they care about the betterment of their fellow humans, it is incumbent upon us to make that a reality using any means possible.

Several societal issues in our communities have caught my interest and I feel a deep need to reach out and try and affect those issues. For instance, as a young boy I gravitated toward my father who was deeply interested in local politics. For my earliest days I remember trailing him from one home to another on the weekends as we spoke with possible candidates for town councils or state offices. We learned about running campaigns, what it was like to be a candidate, and how these people and this process could shape the future of a community. Once my wife and I purchased a house and settled down into our hometown of Lincoln, Rhode Island, I decided it was time to begin getting involved politically. I met my local elected and appointed officials, learned about local issues, and began volunteering my time to various boards and agencies here in town.

As Eleven Limited began to grow more successful, I saw the need to balance the time I was dedicating to the things I felt were important in the community with the money I had available to me through Eleven Limited. I began to see that where I couldn't donate my time, I could donate money.

For instance, in 2007, Eleven Limited was proud to sponsor two scholarships to Ocean State Action's New Voices campaign institute. This program teaches participants how they can become politically active on several levels. What was nice about this program was that it was fairly inexpensive for us to donate the money that would be used for these two scholarships. We set aside several hundreds of dollars that would be used to pay for two female minority activists to attend the institute. The wonderful thing about this was that two women walked out of that seminar with the knowledge needed to run for office or to help other people run for office some day. Those are the kinds of people who can change public policy here at the local level, at the state level, and perhaps even at the federal level.

Show me the money? No . . . show me the commitment.

But it's not all about money and it is certainly not all about donating money. It's about the company's ability to balance a sustained commitment to giving both financial assets as well as time and service assets. And the opportunity to give your time presents itself in the strangest places.

For instance, one time last year I was at the gym during lunchtime working on the treadmill grinding through my daily exercise routine. Around noon, I happened to glance up at the midday news program playing on a television suspended from the ceiling. Here in Rhode Island, "Tuesday's

Child" is a section of Tuesday's mid-day newscast that helps one of our local agencies place children who are up for adoption. That day I looked up and saw one of the most beautiful little girls I had ever seen in my life. While the announcer told her story, this sweet little girl danced and danced — all the while laughing and smiling.

While I knew there was no way we could adopt this young child, I did think to myself, "There must be another way I can help." So I went home, thought about it, and then went to their website. It looked to me like they could use some help in this area. So the next day I contacted Adoption Rhode Island and asked them if they needed a webmaster.

Wouldn't you know it, their webmaster had just decided to accept another job at a different company and they now had no one to watch over the website. This seemed like a win-win situation. I volunteered my services as an interim webmaster and was able to help them out until they were able to hire a new graphic artist who also works as their webmaster. It was a small thing. It didn't take much time and didn't take any money, but I was happy. Every single time I had to update their website, I thought about that little girl dancing on the mid-day news and I said to myself in this small way I'm able to help her, or other children like her.

Sharing our giving story

Is it important for us to share our story with others? Actually I hadn't even given it much thought until I was asked to write a chapter for this book. Since then I've been giving this concept a great deal more thought and I believe that it actually is important to share our giving stories. Upon reflection I've begun to think that by telling people about our giving we can show them that they too can give back. There does not need to be a great deal of cost involved in a giving program. By telling stories like mine and others in this book, companies can see that giving is absolutely doable. So in essence, perhaps telling our giving story is also a bit of strategic business philanthropy.

Measuring success — Are metrics critical to a company's giving program?

For any business to be successful, it has to be able to measure exactly what success means. In the sense that our giving program furthers our brand in the marketplace, I can tell that our program is successful. In the circles where I travel, I hear that people know our name, Eleven Limited, and know of our works. However, we do not strive to compete with any of our peers in our efforts to give. We simply look at our organization and its resources in an effort to develop a giving plan that is meaningful to our business and to the communities we serve.

It's important to note, I think, that our giving program brings us no tangible results or benefits. Yes, our brand is strengthened in the marketplace and the elusive "good will" is strong, but we never started this with the intent of getting something from our giving aside from the knowledge that we're doing the best we can to make a better community.

So, I actually don't have any metric for measuring how successful our giving program is. It's more visceral than measurable. However, there was a time a few years back when my older daughter Maggie, while writing a school paper, mentioned me as one of the people she looked up to. She mentioned the fact that I often give back to my community and she mentioned my active involvement in the community. When I read that paper my heart seemed to grow a bit and my resolve to continue along this path was deepened. That kind of reward is priceless.

Giving back — To create a better society we have to get our hands dirty.

If I had advice to pass along to different companies that are thinking about starting a philanthropy program, I would tell them, "Just do it!" There are many ways to help our communities, there are many ways to help our non-profit organizations, and there are many ways to make things better. All we really have to do is to commit ourselves to this and not to lose sight of the importance of what we're doing. There are a whole set of mechanics that need to go along with a giving program and certainly others throughout this book will mention some of those. But for me, giving is more a matter of the heart. And that's the way it shall remain.

—**Timothy E. McMahon**, Creative Director of Eleven Limited, LLC

Eleven Limited is a small design firm with expertise in web design, print design, and web hosting. Since our inception, we've worked with scores of businesses and individuals. Our tagline is simple, "We're passionate about your business." What does that mean? It's simple — this statement goes to our core belief that you and your business are the most important client we have. We are a small design firm with absolutely no intention of becoming a large design firm. With that maxim in mind, we are selective about the projects we take on. We focus on small to mid-sized businesses that don't have the time or expertise to develop a website or print products that support their overall marketing communications plan.

Contact Information

Eleven Limited is headquartered in Lincoln, Rhode Island. Visit us on the web at **www.elevenlimited.com.**

CHAPTER

10

Process Prodigy, Inc.

Have You Seen My Silver Lining?

How Giving Can Be Simple, Easy and So Rewarding

I remember the exact moment that I realized I was an optimist. It was January 17, 1994. It was early, not even 6 a.m. I had just been violently shaken awake by the Northridge, California earthquake. After scrambling out of my pitch-black bedroom in my nightgown, I found myself outside, shivering in the cold with my roommate, her boyfriend, and a rather hysterical neighbor. In a calm and soothing voice I reassured my neighbor that everything was okay because we weren't injured, we weren't even bleeding. Then it happened, I said it, "Just think, if it was this bad here, how must it have been for those poor people at the epicenter?" I learned a few days later that we, in fact, were those poor people at the epicenter.

The big a-ha about being an optimist came to me when I realized that I just managed to make the best out of what was truly a dire situation. They say every cloud has a silver lining and I had just discovered mine.

It was a little less than 6 years later that I lost that silver lining. At the time I was working for a rapidly growing company where I had 5 jobs all at the same time. One of the newer employees asked me one day what my position was and my answer was, "What day is it?" One day I focused on one set of items, the next day something totally different. I loved it. It had lots of variety and it was a great learning experience. One evening I found myself working late and I didn't want to fight the Los Angeles traffic to go home and eat dinner by myself. I called my parents and invited myself to dinner (after all that's where the food is). After letting myself into the house

I yelled, "Hello, it's me, I'm here." My mom was in the back and she called me over. I still remember the moment. She was getting ready to do the laundry, holding a big pile of dirty socks in her arms she looked at me and proclaimed, "I'm fine."

You know you're in trouble when the conversation starts off, I'm fine.

"Yeah," I said questioning her.

"I just want you to know that I'm fine. It's nothing. I'm sure I'm fine, but I found a lump and I'm going to the doctor," she said pointing to her breast. "It's been there since I was a little girl so I'm sure it's nothing, but I'm going to have it checked out. I just wanted you to know so you weren't surprised or thought I was hiding something from you."

"Okay, are you sick?" I asked still trying to digest what she had just said.

"No, I'm fine. Really, I feel fine. I'm sure it's nothing. Like I said the lump has been there most of my life, it's just changed so I'm going in."

Denial is a really good place to live. I lived there for about a week until the day the phone call came and denial kicked me right out the door. Her voice was calm, but her sense of inner peace was replaced by fear. It was almost like having to say it out loud to her eldest child made it real to her for the first time.

"The biopsy is back and it's cancer. I'm sick. I am going to need you. Can you come?" She said in almost a monotone fashion.

I don't think I've ever been so terrified. For the first time since I was a child I broke into uncontrollable, inconsolable tears. That phone call was 100 times more terrifying than the shaking of the 6.7 earthquake.

Her diagnosis was severe. She was looking at the removal of her breasts, eight rounds of chemotherapy, and weeks of radiation treatment. Was she going to die? None of us knew and we were all scared. Suddenly she was scheduled for a stream of surgeries. They were so frequent that I had claimed a specific spot in the hospital waiting room as my own. On the rare occasion when we would come in and some unknowing soul had the Gaul to sit in my seat, I was angry.

My friends were wonderful. They did everything they could to support me. I just didn't know what I needed. Until that moment I had not known that it was possible to be scarred, angry, depressed and in denial — all at the same time. I was truly lost. I remember being at the doctor's office for my own check-up. After getting off the scale the nurse said, "Wow, you lost 12 pounds, what have you been doing?"

"My mom got cancer."

It came out much meaner than I had meant it to, but it was clear to me in that moment that my silver lining wasn't just missing, I had totally forgotten about it.

After her first breast was removed I remember going home, stripping down, and looking at myself in the mirror. It had never occurred to me to be grateful for my body parts. I stared at my naked chest wondering how I might look without a breast, what it would feel like if it was ever me. Then my thoughts turned to her: what she must be feeling having to deal with the loss, the physical pain of the amputation, and the remaining fear that it might not work and she could still die.

I hadn't even realized I was crying until a tear rolled off my face and landed, ironically, on my breast. For the first time I realized I had been taking a lot for granted and that there was so much to appreciate my body, my relationship with my parents, my amazing circle of friends . . . and then it hit me. There is no such thing as forever and if you want something you have to go out and get it. And get it now. A faint flicker of that silver lining was being to come back.

The Shift

Although I have never had a baby myself, my mom loves to tell me the story about the huge burst of energy she got right before she gave birth to me and how the same thing happened before my brother was born. All of a sudden I felt myself energized. Looking back, I accomplished in six months what many take 10 or 20 years to do. I decided to quit my job to pursue my dreams of opening a business. My brother who had been living in Texas moved back to Los Angeles and became a permanent resident in my guest room. I ended a long-term relationship that had become just a routine for both him and me. Then I packed my bags and went traveling through Europe for a month. And that was only the beginning.

They Made Me Walk

Fast forward a few years. My mom made it through the surgery, the chemo, and the radiation, and was living happily in remission. We were all breathing again. My business was off and running and those same friends who had been there to hold my hand through the though times invited me to walk to raise money for breast cancer research.

It was exciting to be able to do something to give back. That first walk I raised about $1000 which at the time seemed like a lot of money. The following year I raised $3000 and the year after that $5000. Not huge amounts of money, but nonetheless they were ever increasing amounts. I figured that my $5000 was certainly better than nothing.

The day of the walk I was actually a little nervous. I didn't know what to expect or what it would be like. The first thing we did when we got to the walk was to register and fill out the name signs they had available. I proudly taped my mom and my aunt's name (who had also fallen victim to breast cancer) to my back. I went into the walk doing it for them. It made me feel proud.

It opened my eyes to a very large community of people who understood what I was feeling and how scared I had been because they had been there too. In a strange way, that walk was healing for me. It gave me something to contribute. Even if it was just one little thing that I could do to make a difference, I no longer had to just sit on the couch and wait. I found a way to take action and that action became my power.

I wanted to be a part of something that was searching for a cure so that my mom and aunt didn't have to suffer anymore. Honestly, it was selfish. I was taking action, but it was all around what it would do for the women I knew and loved. I wanted it just for them. It wasn't about the bigger picture of people everywhere.

The Bigger Picture

When I started focusing on the entire world around me and stopped paying attention to just the world around me it was as if someone turned the lights on. Suddenly I was back in my office taking that phone call where she first told me she was sick. The voices of the people I had worked with appeared in my head, "my mother had it," "my wife is in treatment," "my sister," etc. Everyone had a story and what really floored me was that in a small office with only about 65 people, almost everyone had a direct connection to someone who had breast cancer. Some were alive and some were gone. And then it happened, my own voice popped up again and said, "See, it's okay, it could be a lot worse." My silver lining was back in full force.

Thousands of people participated in that walk. Hundreds of them were survivors. But there were an even bigger number of people who were walking in memory of someone. It was pretty overwhelming. I fought back tears, realizing again how lucky I was. Even though my mom and later my aunt had certainly been through a horrible ordeal, they were still here. I could still hug them, still laugh with them, still dream about the future with them.

One family who was not so lucky had huge posters of their young family member made. She was very young, probably in her early twenties, and she was gone. Suddenly I was concerned for all women and not just the ones in my own life. I was inspired to make a difference, I just didn't know how.

The Search

It's funny how when you finally open your eyes you see all the possibilities in front of you. At a business dinner I met a woman who was involved with a foundation that was geared towards raising money for cancer treatment. I got involved with the organization and handled a variety of jobs for about a year. I went to meetings. I helped design the backend of their website. I helped with the organization and planning of a monthly mixer. I worked in their corporate office setting up new members. It felt good to feel apart of something that was aimed at making a difference. But after about a year, I found that it was time for me to move on and look for other ways to contribute.

So the search continued. I walked again. I dressed up and went to some swanky charity events. I talked to my mom. All things that made me feel connected to the cause and therefore making a difference.

Connecting the Dots

As my business continued to grow, I was inspired to find a way to tie my need to participate in taking action with the business that had become my baby.

I figured there was some specific "way" that people do this. I was confused about who to give to and how to give it. Where would the money come from? Did I ask for it? Give my own? Would it be enough? I found myself questioning myself so much that for awhile I just did nothing.

Then one day I bought a pink candle and it hit me. The candle was a special candle. A portion of the proceeds were donated to the cause. My first thought was a mistake I believe many small business owners make. I figured since my company wasn't a mega-conglomerate billion dollar organization that I was just too small to do a campaign that would raise funds.

But I was wrong. I remembered that initial $1000 I raised for the first walk. I figured that any amount, no matter how big or how small would be worth it. Any amount I could come up with would give me that personal satisfaction of knowing I was taking action and besides everyone has to start somewhere.

Now that I was raring to go I realized I just needed to pick an organization to contribute to and do something. I did a Google search for "Breast Cancer Charities" and got more than 1,500,000 results. I don't know specifically why I chose Susan G. Komen for the Cure. Maybe it was because I cried when I read the story of Susan Komen. Maybe it was because they have really good branding and I'd seen their name over and over again. Maybe it was because they came up near the top of the list of 1,500,000. I guess what I'm trying to say here is that there was no scientific or strategic reasoning behind my choice, I just picked them.

I learned from my earlier days of volunteer work that participating and working hands on was really rewarding, but it was also very time consuming. After spending several years learning to leverage my time and resources, I made a conscious decision to find something that didn't involve a large block of time, but supplied the same feeling of giving that I had experienced.

The Plan

What seemed to make the most business sense to me was to use, as a model, a program I had already seen be successful. After all, why reinvent the wheel? I started looking around at what the larger companies did to see how I could adapt their methods to my personal situation and company. I narrowed my choices down to a couple of options; donate a percentage of proceeds from product and service sales to Susan G. Komen for the Cure or create a specific event where I brought in a large sponsor to cover costs and then donate a piece of the event's profits to the charity. The latter was actually a technique I learned from a colleague. It seems that those large mega-conglomerate billion dollar companies get some nice tax breaks when their money goes to support charities. So working with the big money, the charity, and my company could be a win-win-win for all. This is something I am still working on. However, since my original desired outcome was to start with something that did not require a lot of time I chose the first option.

The next step was to decide a time frame. This one was easy for me since October is Breast Cancer Awareness month, I chose October 1 through October 31. Talk about your no-brainer.

At the beginning of the month, my technology team added some graphics to my website announcing that for the month of October 2007, 5 percent of all proceeds would be donated to Susan G. Komen for the Cure.

We then sent out a series of email announcements to my mailing list telling them what was going on and how they could participate. The total cost of the campaign was about an hour of tech time and about an hour of my time writing the announcement. This was very inexpensive to set up and took almost no time to manage. Yet, I was left with an incredibly feeling of empowerment because I was taking action.

When all was said and done, on the business side of things, the announcements increased my product sales for the month, which of course meant a larger check for Susan G Komen for the Cure. Who knew I'd be so happy to write a check to give away money. Giving and knowing you are supporting a worthy cause makes you feel really good. On the personal side of things, I was touched by the number of people who wrote me to me to share their own stories and to simply just say thank you for helping.

—Beth Schneider, President/CEO, Process Prodigy, Inc.

Process Prodigy, Inc. is a group of operations consultants that helps entrepreneurs cut back work hours, extend vacations, eliminate wasted time, and make more money. Our tools and techniques have helped entrepreneurs increase productivity by as much as 600 percent, and revenues by as much as 250 percent.

Contact Information

www.processprodigy.com

CHAPTER

11

O'Neill Pine Company

Giving Back through Business Tithing

Eight years of hour-long commutes gives a person a lot of time for creative thinking. The opportunity to put that creative thinking into action came in 1996 when my wife and I had a chance to establish our branch of the family business. By that time we already had some innovative ideas on how to incorporate our values into our business plan:

1. The company would tithe net income.
2. The company would tithe employee time; 10 percent of each employee's paid work hours were to be in service of non-profit organizations.
3. The company would help establish and then pay the operational expenses of Evergreen Charitable Trust as an integral part of our business plan.

O'Neill Pine Company (OPC) started operations on January 1, 1996. We are a spin-off from Hemphill-O'Neill Company. Both companies continue today in their third generation of family management. OPC is primarily a timber company, with some diversified investments to provide corporate financial stability. In 2000, OPC forest practices were certified by the Forest Stewardship Council (FSC). FSC certification requires companies to meet high economic, social, and environmental standards. You can learn more about O'Neill Pine Company at **www.opineco.com**.

Why Giving Back Is Important

We believe our Christian faith calls us to give. We believe everything we have has been given to us by God. We think we have the greatest deal in the world that we are only called to give back 10 percent as a tithe. We acknowledge there are other Christians who do not feel a call to give 10 percent, there are Christians who give more than 10 percent, and there are many non-Christians who are also very generous. For our family, giving back through our business is an expression of our faith.

The long-term nature of our timber business encourages us to give. We harvest trees that were planted by prior generations. We plant trees that will be harvested by future generations. In the same way that we plant trees for the benefit of my children and grandchildren we also tithe — planting seeds of benefit for the community that my children and grandchildren will live in.

The founding father of our business was Robert "Harold" O'Neill. He found success in business relatively late in life. Before that success there were failures, but he rebounded. He loved to wrap presents and give things away. He felt strongly about the importance of being in business for yourself. He tracked and understood business cycles. The values of Grandpa O'Neill are reflected in our programs to give back to the community.

None of us, no matter how great our resources or insurance policies, are more than a few unfortunate life turns away from needing the help of our communities to survive. I like to think of myself as very self-reliant, but in truth we all benefit from a strong community support system.

How Our Program Works

The company gives 10 percent of its net income each year to non-profit organizations. Most of our contributions go to support the work of Evergreen Charitable Trust, but OPC also supports:

- **Checkbooks for Kids — Community Foundation of Southwest Washington**. The principal of each grade school in our timberland area receives a checkbook from the Community Foundation. The principal can write checks against the account to meet student needs, with no paperwork or approval necessary. The accounts have been used for student fees, eye glasses, field trips, and even alarm clocks for kids who get up alone after their parents have already gone to work.

- **Operation School Bell — Assistance League of Salem.** The program helps enhance the self-esteem of children in need by providing them with new school clothes, shoes, and a hygiene kit. Through requests from school counselors, over 2,500 children are clothed annually.
- **Building Fund — Salem Area Chamber of Commerce.** We are one of many companies that contributed far beyond dues to support the mission of the Chamber.

Each employee is expected to work 10 percent of his or her paid work time in service of non-profit organizations. Thus, an employee who works thirty hours in a week will be expected to serve another three paid hours for a non-profit organization. This work requirement is written into our job descriptions. We recruit with this provision as a clear employee expectation and we evaluate employees on this standard just as we do on any other performance expectation.

The company reserves the right to disallow service to certain non-profit organizations, but we have never exercised that right. Rather than try to direct the service, we allow employees to find ways to serve the community that they feel passionate about. Our employees have shown great enthusiasm for a variety of non-profit organizations.

Normal, full-time work at our company is a thirty-hour work week. Another company value is to allow employees a life outside of work. We are careful not to let charitable hours create overtime hours.

Schools and churches have been the most frequent beneficiaries of our employees' service, but some other service is noteworthy:

- **Girl Scouts** — one of our employees coordinated which scouts and their parents got to sell outside of which grocery stores during which hours. Not a job for the faint of heart.
- **Children's Advocate** — providing advocacy services for kids who through no fault of their own are dragged into the justice system. Sometimes this was as simple as being just a safe friend to talk to.

- **Master Gardener** — an educational program that then requires graduates to teach others. Two of our employees participated in this program, and then provided a hands-on learning experience about seeds for first-graders.

In addition to reporting paid non-profit service hours, we ask our employees to voluntarily report additional unpaid community service hours. A particularly gratifying part of this program is that typically, unpaid volunteer hours are three or four times the amount of paid non-profit service hours.

OPC has shared these plans with companies we work with frequently and encouraged them to adopt similar provisions. We know that one company fully adopted the provisions. Another did not adopt the whole package but gives charitable contributions that they probably would not be giving if they did not know of our company policies.

Evergreen Charitable Trust was established in 1998 to help individuals and organizations create charitable endowment funds. Evergreen breaks endowment funds into two parts. The basis is the amount contributed by donors into the fund. The basis will stay forever as part of the trust. Earnings from investing the funds provide the distributable portion of the endowment fund. Donors or their representatives can advise Evergreen on which non-profit organizations they want to receive distributions from the endowment fund.

Evergreen provides services similar to larger community foundations, with two significant differences. First, Evergreen has no minimum starting amount. Larger organizations know that small advised funds are not efficient to work with. Evergreen is willing to help people build charitable habits with small funds.

The second significant difference is that Evergreen charges no fees or loads for its normal services. It can do this because its operational expenses are paid for by OPC. Evergreen can proudly say that 100 percent of all contributions go to charitable causes.

Endowment funds are not for everyone. OPC encourages anyone interested in charitable endowment funds to visit the Evergreen Charitable Trust web site at **www.evertrust.org**.

Our charitable policies are very expensive. Especially in lean business years, we talk about reducing our generosity. There are thousands of ways for companies to contribute to their communities. We are not locked into forever doing what we are doing today. We hope that as our company continues and evolves it will always have charitable provisions which fit that particular stage of the company's life.

The last sentence of our company Essence Statement is:

> There is more to life than making money! We have values that are more important than profits. Work is a way to honor God.

That statement summarizes our reasons for giving back.

— **Richard Pine,** President, O'Neill Pine Company

O'Neill Pine Company grows trees in Southwest Washington. We produce a sustained yield harvest of one million board feet per year. To find out more about the company see **www.opineco.com**.

- Lewis County Farm Forestry Chapter Award for Forest Stewardship 2001
- Oregon Business Magazines Best Small Business to Work for in Oregon 2001
- Austin Family Business Program, Top Female owned business in Oregon 2000

Contact Information

O'Neill Pine Company
1640 Liberty SE
Salem, OR 97302
rpine@opineco.com
503-315-2400

CHAPTER

12

Elinvar

Giving Back

A mother should never underestimate the impact she has on her children. When I reflect on the forces that drive me I believe that how my mother lived her life . . . and how she died . . . converged to influence the life I have chosen to live.

My mother died when I was 31 years old. Up until her diagnosis of cancer, I had led my life without any real sense of purpose. I had married, divorced, and had a successful career as a CPA. But I had made the decisions that created the first years of my adulthood without much thought to the world outside of my own.

The perpetual volunteer and community leader, my mother postponed her critical surgery by a week so she could complete the hospital fundraiser she was leading that year. The classic post–World War II wife and mother, she had not held a paying job outside of our home but found her fulfillment from her community activities.

Now, before I give you an inaccurate picture of "June Cleaver" I must tell you that all was not rosy in her life. So when she died an early and miserable death I stopped for the first time to ask, what is this all about? How can a good person have such misery in her life and in her death? My mother's gift to me was a determination that I would face my death, whenever that time came, knowing that I had made the most of my time on this planet. Thank you Momma!

Fast forward a few years and I transplanted myself to a new town (Raleigh, North Carolina) and a new career in executive search. In less than

2 years I owned a home and had a small ownership interest in the firm I was working for. I was humbled by my good fortune. I recognized that it was time for me to give back to a community that had given so much to me. At the same time, I was looking for ways to develop professionally and to grow my business. For those reasons my volunteer work over the years has been comprised of two tracks — professional associations and non-profit support related to my passions outside of my work.

As a former CPA recruiting financial professionals for companies, I operated in two worlds — the financial world and the human resource industry. For that reason, I joined professional associations for both and held board positions in several related organizations.

My reasons for these volunteer positions were self-serving. I was able to grow professionally and I felt more comfortable meeting new people if I was serving in a specific role. However, I learned over the years that my underlying motivation is that I really get my kicks by seeing other people progress in realizing their dreams. And these volunteer positions helped me do that.

I especially liked to match speakers with program needs for these organizations. It was like planning a party and then holding your breath to see if anyone would come!

Then, in May 2001, I visited an organization I thought would help me meet CEO's. Instead I met the volunteer president of an association that badly needed help. He invited me to join the board and we set out to revive a chapter that was on its last leg. We identified some more volunteers and spent the next few years working to re-start an organization focused on corporate growth — an interesting challenge after 9/11 and during a brutal recession.

This effort led to a great series of board positions, new friendships, and very rewarding work that has affected many of our volunteers in a very positive way. While I cannot trace any one client to my work in this association, I am certain that it has benefited my business and my professional growth tremendously.

My non-profit service also started around my second year living in Raleigh. It is amazing how doors open just when you start to look for them.

I had just mentioned to my business partner that I wanted to find some way to get involved in the community when I learned of a project for kids who were at risk of dropping out of school!

What I didn't know about volunteering was if you do it they will let you! The next thing I knew I was co-leading the project with a great woman who was equally passionate about helping these kids. This first project led me to a path I have been on for 18 years and counting.

But first, you need to know about the other "door" that opened for me around the same time. I heard from a friend about a local class being taught for people who wanted to become clowns. My younger brother was a self-taught clown in high school but I had never been inclined to do anything like this. I guess the time was right because I signed up and created "Bubbles" the clown.

As life would have it my teacher turned out to be my future husband! This is not germane to this story but was certainly a significant event.

Around this time I happened to hear about Patch Adams who was taking groups of volunteers to clown in the former Soviet Union. I had always been fascinated by the USSR so I thought — why not? Little did I know what a life-changing experience this would be.

We traveled to Moscow, St. Petersburg, and Estonia in the fall of 1991. There were about 25 clowns in our group; most were doctors, and I dare say none of us were the same after this trip. We met the most amazing people, performed in the Moscow circus, and were welcomed into the homes of many Russians who had no idea where their next meal was coming from but who managed to prepare a feast for us.

For me, the defining moments were with the children. As a new clown I was shy about performing so I wandered the hospital halls and found the children who were too ill to come to the performance. "Bubbles" sat with their mothers who also served as their nurses, and through these special moments I reconnected with my heart — the heart I had been guarding for most of my life.

When I returned home I decided it was time for me to become a hospice volunteer so I signed up for the training class. I managed to complete the class but realized that I was not ready to do the work. My mother's death was still too fresh.

During Clown College we were encouraged to join a non-profit group of clowns. Through this association I suddenly had all kinds of opportunities to reach out in the community — from nursing homes to inner-city kids. We were someplace different every weekend. It was great!

As a person who enjoys many different things I greatly enjoyed the variety, but I had a busy job and a new family (my husband brought two great kids with him). So, I soon decided that I needed to pick one area to focus on.

After some thought it seemed clear that directing my community service efforts toward supporting kids who were not getting the attention they needed to be successful in school was the right direction for me to go. This was a clear passion that I could trace back to my freshman year in college.

My first year in college was spent at a small school located in a mill town in South Carolina. For a class project my theater class went to the local elementary school to work with the kids. We brought paper grocery bags and crayons to the school and helped them make masks to serve as costumes. I will never forget the little girl who was pretending to iron because she had no imagination for anything beyond what she had seen her mother do.

It had also become obvious when we were working on the job-shadowing program for at-risk kids in Raleigh that our school system had no focus on helping this population of students. The need was great and talented kids were getting left behind.

Finally, I reasoned that because I was in the human resource profession, helping more kids get a good education was clearly related to making sure we had good employees to hire, even though it would be few years before these efforts paid off.

Fortunately my business partner was supportive of my volunteer work. I met a wonderful woman (who is now a dear friend) who was leading the local Communities in Schools (CIS) organization. I joined the board and served that organization for about 8 years. This board was comprised of many business leaders in our community so the benefits to me and my company were also there. While I do not believe you should volunteer with an expectation of getting something back in return, I think you always receive more than you give.

Over the years we hired several employees who had thought about teaching as a profession but had picked business instead. We were able to connect them with volunteer mentoring programs through CIS, giving them a great outlet for their desires to teach. Serving on a board with leaders from larger organizations gave me the opportunity to learn from other business people. And I believe our community service has set us apart from many of our competitors.

During these years I moved up to president of our company and purchased the company when my partner retired. I have always encouraged our employees to volunteer — if they want to. And if they do, I tell them it must be something they really care about. Of course this can be a double-edged sword. When you really care it is hard to turn it off!

There have been many times when I lost sleep over an issue happening with a non-profit I was serving and weeks when I spent much more time on my volunteer role than on my "day job." When the recession hit our industry in 2002 our market really suffered because our economy had been so technology-focused. For the first year I had to step back my volunteer efforts while I refocused our organization. When we did not have the funds to financially support some of our favorite causes we donated our office space for fund-and-friend-raisers and called on clients for financial support for these events.

It was around this time that a friend of mine asked me to help a new principal at one of our middle schools. She had inherited a staff that was clearly unhappy and she wanted focus groups conducted to determine what she could do to motivate and retain her teachers.

The focus groups revealed that recognizing the efforts of the teachers and administrators who spent many extra hours with school activities would be a good direction for the principal to take. We brought together a group of business people to assist her with implementing this plan. Two years later one of the administrators who was ready to leave the school and the profession at the time of the first focus group gave a testimonial about how the principal's leadership had kept him in both.

When it was time to re-engage my volunteer efforts, I realized that the landscape for public education in our community had been changing significantly. In particular, a new superintendent and school board had brought attention and resources to support our less fortunate students and great progress had been made. I had also learned that making a real difference in public education called for changes in policy and I was ready to see if I could help in this arena.

A few years ago I joined the board of our local education fund which serves as an advocate for excellence in our public schools. Working on this board, serving on committees that report to and advise our school board, and volunteering at a local middle school have all served to deepen my understanding of the challenges facing our public education system. As we experience increased competition in a global economy, the need for a sense of urgency to meet these challenges seems clearer every day.

While our community has made great progress in the years I have followed my passion by trying to help in my small way, I am daunted by the thought that it has been 18 years! How many kids have we missed? This is a whole generation that has been lost forever. These kids are in our prisons when they could be in our work force. Public education is the foundation for our democracy, but we are spending billions in other countries while we are continuing to debate what to do in our own communities.

That is the thought that drives me and the many great volunteers, teachers, and community leaders who dedicate their lives to this cause. When I feel discouraged I look around and see the fight continuing and that gets me back on track. Or, as Bubbles the clown, I look into the eyes of a child and I see so much promise that I cannot give up!

Last year my company donated our services to lead the search for a new president for this organization. An incredible candidate was introduced by one of our board members and we have all been amazed at the progress she has made in just one year. While my company cannot take credit for this great hire, we were proud to be a part of this success and believe we had an important role in the process.

Over the years we have donated our search services to other non-profits in our community. We also provide direct financial assistance in the form of donations and because we know so many people and organizations in our community we make other connections as well.

Our philosophy of giving back is ingrained in who we are as an organization. It affects every decision we make in our business dealings as well as in our community activities. I do not think you can separate the two worlds. As our team has matured over the years we have become clearer about these values. Because of that, we deliberately attract new employees who share our values and they give back with the same passion and care I expect of myself.

Our company's mission is to make a difference. That has been our vision statement for over 13 years. We are a small company with five employees. But we have demonstrated that a small group of people can make a big difference. My favorite movie is "It's a Wonderful Life" with Jimmy Stewart. If we can know as we leave this planet that by our being here, people had happier lives, then it was all worth while.

— **Patti Gillenwater**, CEO, Elinvar

Elinvar is an executive search firm serving top companies based in the Raleigh, North Carolina area. Founded in 1986, Elinvar is well known in our community for our high ethics, commitment to excellence and community spirit. We have a unique business model that aligns our efforts and values with those of our clients and candidates. With this collaborative model we make great things happen for the people we serve!

Contact Information

www.elinvar.com

CHAPTER

13

Studio N

A Giving Habit Becomes a Giving Principle

I began my giving program almost by mistake, just as I started my business almost by mistake 19 years ago. I had worked in book publishing as an editor and production manager, responsible for helping turn manuscripts into published books. In 1987, my boss told me that hard times were forcing him to close the company, but he asked me to stay on part-time to help him close the business. This took several months, and I began taking in freelance copy editing assignments to supplement my income.

It was a time of transition for the book publishing and design industry. Personal computers were making it possible for individuals to produce documents with very little investment; a typesetting machine used to cost upwards of $10,000 and now you could do graphic design and layout with just a few thousand dollars invested in a computer and software.

I soon became more interested in graphic design than in copy editing. After a brief stint working for a book production company in Pennsylvania, I hung out my shingle as a full-time graphic designer, taking advantage of a recession to pick up business from companies who couldn't afford expensive high-end design firms and were willing to put up with my learning curve.

During my first years in business I wasn't thinking much about philanthropy; it was too tough trying to make ends meet. Sometimes collecting a bill was harder than doing the work in the first place. One time I spent 4 hours designing a flier, charged the client $100, and then had to collect the fee $25 at a time by making personal visits to his store. On my third visit, the client was "a little short" and asked me to return the next week. I gave up on the remaining $50, reasoning that times must be a lot harder for him than for me.

My giving usually consisted of giving smaller businesses, artists, and musicians a break because they couldn't afford a higher fee. I often worked for free when asked, but I did not have a philosophy of giving. I viewed service and community organizations with suspicion, thinking that people joined such organizations for self-serving reasons.

It was for a self-serving reason that I joined the board of directors of our local Chamber of Commerce. Simply put, I wanted to get more customers. This worked well for my business — I served for three years on the board of directors, threw myself into project after project, received invaluable mentoring from many people, and got more customers too. Along the way, I began, slowly, to gain respect for those who gave because of an inner drive or principle.

During these years I married and had a son. A few weeks before my son turned two, I was upstairs in my office working on a project when I received an instant message from a client. The World Trade Center had been hit by a plane. My husband and I spent the day in shock. After an hour or so, I said, "I may as well keep working — I don't know what else to do." My husband took my son out for a walk to the ATM to get some cash in case we had to leave suddenly. He called me on his cell phone on the way back to say hello, and I remember barking at him: "They're saying not to call on cell phones! Just come home!" I implored him to stay home from work, which he did. We kept turning on the TV to see if we were in any more danger, and turning it off as quickly as we could so that our son wouldn't see the violent images that played over and over again.

I am not the first person who has been galvanized into some kind of action by tragedy, nor will I be the last. I had what pop psychologists call a "no-option response." I felt that I had to do something, no matter how small. So I invented "Scone Day." I prepared a leaflet explaining that the next Saturday would be "Scone Day" in our neighborhood. For $1.25 per scone, I invited my neighbors to pre-order scones. I asked that they write out their checks to the Red Cross and drop them off at my house with their order forms. Then on the morning of "Scone Day," I would deliver fresh home-baked scones in time for their second cup of coffee if not their first.

The response was tremendous. Even though I only did the Scone Day on my one little street, my neighbors ordered dozens and dozens of scones, ome of them overpaid by quite a bit, and my mother sent in a check for $100 because she was proud of me. On the morning of Scone Day, I got up early and baked the scones — four different recipes. I had an old double oven dating from 1968 and it cooked the scones unevenly, burning some of them on the bottom. I filed the bottoms down with a cheese grater. No one complained — the scones were delicious even if some were misshapen and many were late. My husband and I piled my son and bags of scones into a little red wagon and went up and down the street delivering our orders.

The following year, my son was in preschool and the school was looking for ways to raise funds. I have never liked the idea of school fundraising companies that sell merchandise and give the school back half of the proceeds . . . people sometimes feel pressured into buying things they don't need, and only half of the money goes to the organization raising funds. So I suggested doing a "Scone Day" for the school. From that point forward, each year I have done a "Scone Day" for causes very big and very small. The year Hurricane Katrina devastated New Orleans, our Scone Day raised over $1200 for the Red Cross's hurricane relief efforts (and I, with lots of help from my best friends, baked over 800 scones in one night).

During these years, my business grew, and my husband and I divorced. Despite the turmoil, I was beginning to formulate a more principled notion of what giving was all about. Rather than giving non-profits a discount mostly for marketing purposes, I began to view the discount — 25 percent of my fees to non-profits whose work aligns with my principles — as a moral imperative. When the U.S. Government sent an "economic stimulus refund," I donated a job to one of my non-profit clients in an amount that corresponded to the refund.

I can rarely afford a cash donation, but I always have at least one pro bono project going on and sometimes more. While in the past I worked for free on most projects I was asked to (often feeling I had succumbed to social pressure), I now have a positive attitude towards my contributions, and have developed some criteria for choosing which causes to support. The most important criterion is effective use of resources. If a non-profit organization or cause is not well-managed, my contribution will be less effective.

I remember one charity event that I had done all the graphics for gratis — logos, posters, response cards, fliers, advertisements, and tickets. I was eager to contribute more to the event, and the organizer mentioned a silent auction. I stayed up all night the night before, painstakingly designing and fabricating a beaded necklace. "They ought to get at least $50 for this," I reasoned as I blinked sleep out of my eyes. When I got to the event, the silent auction had been cancelled for lack of interest and they raffled off my necklace as a door prize. Their organization netted $0 from the raffle; the lucky winner was a man who looked completely bewildered by his sudden gain.

Fortunately I learned from that mistake. The next time I helped with an event, I chose a group that listened respectfully to my ideas. I donated the graphics for free, a value of approximately $750. But my most important contribution was to suggest that the organization seek some named sponsors for the event. So board members contacted a local hospital and supermarket who had relatively large budgets and offered them named gift opportunities — adding $1500 to the event's take.

Another criterion for giving is gratitude. I don't mean that the organization needs to be slavishly grateful to you for what you have done or embarrass you with overblown expressions of thanks. I simply mean that they need to appreciate what you have done. Now this runs contrary to an idea I have heard expressed in my church — that we should give in ways that are unrecognized as often as possible. I do agree with this idea and I like to think that I have done some of this, although our church's pastor has a way of finding out my good deeds even when I try to conceal them. However, if you are contributing to a cause or an organization that is trying to effect positive change, the best place to put your efforts is where they will be leveraged the best. The board members who listened respectfully to my idea did so because they were grateful for my work, and thus more receptive to my ideas. They raised extra money for their organization because they had an "attitude of gratitude." They know how to utilize the gifts that come their way.

A third principle I have followed is to go where I am led. A couple I am acquainted with asked me to help with some work for an arts organization they started. I didn't know much about the arts organization but I knew I wanted to become better friends with this couple — so I signed on. Not only have I gained friendship, but I have found a way to become better connected to the cultural life within my hometown.

A fourth principle is to apply basic marketing savvy to the gifts you give, so that they can raise as much money as possible. This principle is seen in many charity auctions, where a gift raises many times the amount it cost the giver. In the case of Scone Day, I wanted the scones to fetch a high price. I have always found it troubling (and perhaps sexist, since baking is seen as women's work) that goods are so under-priced at most bake sales. You have to pay over $3.00 for a brownie at Starbucks, so why should you pay only 50 cents for a similar brownie at a bake sale? With Scone Day I figured out how to charge a premium price for the same amount of sugar and cholesterol. My scones now fetch $1.50 apiece because the novelty of having them delivered in a red wagon adds value and positions them as premium goods.

Finally, I try to leave enough room in my life to respond to events that demand an immediate response. If one of your children is hurt, you drop everything and get care for the child. One day a few years ago, our family woke up to find some racist hate literature on the front lawn. For some reason the most frightening part of it was that it had been wrapped around a small stone so that someone could toss it out of a car window and keep going. All around our neighborhood, these little bundles littered people's lawns. My son was in kindergarten at the time, and had almost learned how to read. Something had to be done right away — our community had been wounded.

So, my husband and I walked around the neighborhood and picked up all the racist trash we could find. Then, I wrote a letter to the local newspaper explaining that hate was not welcome in our town. I went up and down the street gathering signatures on the letter. Finally, I wrote out a check for $500 to the city to help implement a "No Place For Hate" initiative that was already in place, but was underfunded. The school department used the money to involve hundreds of children in a curriculum that culminated in a city-wide exhibit of pictures and stories. Did I get much billable work done that first day? No. Where did I get the $500? I had it earmarked for a new leather jacket and Christmas gifts for my clients. My clients received a letter explaining about the donation, and I still wear my old shredded leather jacket. But I was fortunate to have the flexibility to respond as I was called to respond.

Many of the stories I hear about giving have to do with religion or spirituality. This is part of my story, too. Both of my parents were atheists, and I was raised with only the barest knowledge of religious tradition. My mother is (and my father was) a deeply good person, passionately committed to peace, social justice, and kindness. My mother, now 75, still works many hours a week volunteering in local political campaigns because she believes in working for a better world. It's just neither of them believed in God, or took me to church.

On one of my Scone Days, I decided to give the proceeds to a local community gospel choir. My boyfriend had been hired to play guitar at their concert. The musical director had brought together a rainbow of people from several different churches, many with little or no musical training, to hold a concert commemorating Black History Month. I was so moved by the concert that I donated the proceeds of my next Scone Day to the choir. Following this, the director asked me to join her church choir. I have been a blues drummer for several years, I love gospel music, and I was dying to sing, so I said yes.

A few months later I had lunch with my pastor. "I don't have the gift of certainty in my faith," I explained. "But I believe that I have been unconsciously trying to follow the Christian path for a few years now. I have made a lot of mistakes in my personal life, but I feel that following Jesus' teachings will help give me the strength and courage I need to do more of what is right." My pastor agreed, and I was baptized earlier this year in front of my new church community and some skeptical friends and family. As I told my stepdaughter (my ex-husband's daughter), "My faith gives me courage and comfort. I promise never to use it to make you, or anyone else I love, uncomfortable. I believe that you have to find your own path and I only pray that it will be true to who you are, and will bring you the courage and comfort that you need."

Participating in church has given me an even stronger sense of purpose about my giving. I now believe that it is our responsibility to give, and now I actively seek out ways to give because of this principle. People in our church provide me a daily example of generosity, digging deep into their pockets, not only for tithes and offerings, but also to fund mission work. I know retired people who work almost full-time as volunteers. I am not sure I could ever come close to their level of giving, but their example is a constant inspiration to me.

As these changes occur in my philosophy of giving, Studio N has, just in recent weeks, become a part-time business. One of my clients offered me a job! I am now working as a marketing associate for a wind energy company. The new job evolved out of a long-term project I was involved in as a consultant, and out of my commitment to wind energy and to sustainable living. While I have enjoyed and benefited from the many associations I have had in my career as a solo business owner, I am even more energized by the opportunity to spend most of my work hours within an industry that I feel is vital to our earthly health.

But my life as a business giver continues. Our company has already supported some of my giving endeavors and will likely continue.

— Naomi Pierce

Studio N is a full-service graphic design, book production, and web development firm.

Contact Information

Studio N
www.studio-n.com

CHAPTER

14

Fearless Living, Inc.

Living is Easy with Eyes Closed[1]

It's not an easy road to live the passion in your heart or to live with your eyes open. Witnessing. Seeing things you want to change, wanting to see differently but don't know if you have the capacity to. Big things. There are so many issues out there to change that as a small business it's easy to feel overwhelmed by the mere scope of it. No, it's much easier to live with eyes closed.

I wanted my life and my business, once I'd made the decision to launch it, to mean something big. I wanted the blood and sweat of my work to not be just about earning a better living but to make a difference.

But what difference? I knew in the vague sense that my business was going to contribute, but to what ends, I'd not determined. There were many causes and issues out there, but nothing that seemed to deeply connect with me. So I launched, without yet knowing my deeper purpose. My eyes closed.

In the beginning, I didn't even have the time to consider options. The daily issues of launching and surviving took all of my attention and effort. Days became months and then became years. I had chosen to go into the fitness business and become a coach and ultimately open my own gym, itself a long-held dream of mine and while I enjoyed what I was doing immensely, and my business was surviving, I hadn't yet found my larger purpose.

[1]"Strawberry Fields," lyrics by John Lennon and Paul McCartney.

Not at all what I had intended. Many others have fallen into the same trap. They too had the best of intentions yet find themselves going through the motions of having a business, but without any great purpose to its existence.

Then something happens. You personally experience or observe something and somehow, it connects with another memory. The two events suddenly become one and it lights a fire, giving birth to your cause. You find your purpose, your why. And both you and your business gain a determination to grow to meet this challenge. To bring about the change you now know to be yours to make.

For me the moment that lit the fire came in 2004 with a television news picture from Fallujah, Iraq. There on the screen in the gym, as I stood watching, was a picture of four burned bodies hanging from a bridge. Four men shot, then dragged through the streets, their bodies hung from the bridge and burned.

And I knew one of those men.

Something snapped in me, or rather, connected to another pivotal moment.

I was lying down in the hospital having my finger stitched after an accident earlier that morning. The door to the ER burst open and in rushed an entire team of medical staff pushing a stretcher, frantic to get the man on it transferred to a table.

They placed the man right next to me and immediately got to work, cutting off his shirt to get at the gunshot wound underneath. I remember the blood, the frantic words from the doctors and nurses working on him, the sounds of the instruments, everything about the moment.

It was an important moment for me.

It was the moment I witnessed the death of a police officer.

And I was only 9 years old.

Here were two men and two different events separated by over 30 years.

Yet somehow, together, they lit a fire in my heart. I now knew my cause and what I and my business needed to do next.

Serving those who serve

I spent every free hour I had over the next few days poring over my business plan. Rewriting and refocusing it toward that newly found purpose. I wove into it an increasing level of contribution that matched the expansion and growth of my business. Growth that I knew would be necessary to do the things I now needed to do. Things I needed to change. Everything fell into place.

The fitness training programs would incorporate a specialized and directed process to help all my clients deal with stress, to feel less overwhelmed by life. My training became more than just physical training. This new process would also have the benefit of helping the military and first responder communities deal with Post Traumatic Stress Disorder, PTSD.

Next would come the creation of systems so that I could duplicate my efforts with the hiring of staff, enabling me to work with and help larger numbers of people. This too would be focused to include not just a range of civilian trainers and coaches but would also include returning vets. Some hale and hearty, others physically injured in recent conflicts.

The people I shared this with thought I was nuts. I was told no one would want to work with vets, especially someone injured. Yes, I knew this would be an issue for some. I was okay with that. But I also have enough respect for myself and for the passion of my business to let those clients go. I do not need to work with everyone. I believed there would be clients who would work with veterans. Who saw these men and women as heroes. Injured or not, their struggles, discipline, and dedication are expressions of the strength of the human heart. So part of my business plan was fine-tuning who my clients would be. I let go of the need to work with everyone. I would only work with people who found the veterans' strength and courage inspiring. Clients who would see the veterans, observe their example, and use it to fuel their inner drive to push through their own challenges and spur themselves to greater success, physically and mentally.

And as my business grew, I would finally be able to add monetary giving to the mix. And not simply blanket checkbook giving. No, my monetary donations would be in support of the larger philanthropy framework I had created. Serving those who serve. So military and first responder communities would be the recipients of my business's monetary giving.

The plan wasn't perfect. The ebb and flow of business and the cycles of the economy did affect the scale of what I could do and the timing of my expansion. Again, days became months became years. Clients wouldn't pay, and challenges with the city jeopardized the survival of my business. There were constant roadblocks to overcome.

Not the least of which were my own self-created ones.

Because up to this point, I'd been a one-man show. But I knew I couldn't stay that way any more. Not only did my business need to grow, so did I.

I had worked so much on my business, but not on me. There was so much more I needed to do on myself.

I went back to my plan. Read it. And understood that I needed to be a part of it too. That I needed to grow personally so I could take on the larger projects I had planned. It became a moment of letting go. It wasn't a comfortable thought. To realize I had been the impediment to success. I had to grow and let go the role of technician, and take on a new and broader role. I couldn't do anything less. My cause required it.

So I let go.

And my personal struggles now had a purpose as well.

I come clean

I've gone back and forth about whether or not to share this with you. But I decided to, not to extract an emotional reaction, for that isn't it's purpose. Rather, I truly want you to understand the difference having a purpose makes to your business, to its success, and to you personally.

For there are struggles in running your own business. And they can seem overwhelming at times. It would be easy to give up. Shut things down. Move on.

Yet with a cause bigger than yourself, it simply won't allow you to give up. It makes you dig deep, find strength and keep surviving. It spurs you to find ways to make it work for too much depends on continuing. Your cause, my cause requires it.

Rather than being a drag on a company, a focused purpose, born from your own passion keeps you going through all the challenges and struggles and long hours. It makes you grow, reach, and expand.

So you see, I'll be honest here. I'm living a lie. Or, I suppose you could say I'm living a story. To all outward appearances my business has survived 9 years. And it's met with success, to the degree it could run with just my efforts. And I'm proud of that. No one, not even my own family, had faith that it would work or last.

But to accomplish my purpose, my business requires more of me and required me to sacrifice.

So when I went to rent the additional square footage I would need to have the space to hire staff and train more clients at one time, I gave up my apartment so that I could free up the funds necessary to afford it, moving into a small corner of the gym itself. To save money, I dumpster dove for office furniture. And thank goodness for eBay and Craig's List because I've purchased more than half the equipment for my gym through those environments. It's kept things afloat.

It's kept my business going. It's kept my passion alive and with it, my hopes to serve those who serve. And there are men and women who came to me for training, bringing their own dreams of serving in the military, police and fire departments who I'm pleased to say are doing just that because I and my business did survive to serve them.

And I am so very grateful for all of it. I am grateful for my clients and the naysayers; for the success and the failure; for the struggles and the challenges.

Every little bit of it.

For I understand now.

Business is about profits with a purpose. I truly believe this. And I also know that I cannot and will not have my business stand for anything less than that ideal. There are some who may understand this and many who may disagree with it, but it doesn't matter. I've found when you are living your passion, and your business is living its purpose, the opinions of others do not matter.

The opinion you hold in your own heart does. I can honestly say that I finish each day proud of what I've done thus far and firm in the belief of what will yet be accomplished serving those who serve.

And I shut the lights out every night, with a smile on my face, and my eyes wide open.

— **David Di Francesco**, founder and owner, Fearless Living, Inc.

Fearless Living, Inc. is dedicated to tackling stress, physical conditioning, and life performance needs of men around the world. From nationally available weekend training clinics, 5 day warrior fitness adventures, coaching programs and seminars to on-site physical training and mental conditioning at his training center, David and his staff have also made their services available to provide training to those who serve in the military and first responder communities and as an adjunct to Post Traumatic Stress Disorder treatment in veterans.

Contact Information

Fearless Living, Inc.
216 The Promenade N. #310
Long Beach, CA. 90802
www.warriorworkout.com

CHAPTER

15

Organized East of the River

Organized Giving

My personal giving began many years ago with the United Way/Combined Health Appeal at my place of employment. At first, I gave to the American Diabetes Association because my mother suffers from diabetes, but then I also began donating to the American Cancer Society after losing a close friend to breast cancer. Members of my department and I often volunteered our time planting gardens and providing manual labor during Day of Caring events. When I started my own business, it was natural to continue the type of giving I had been providing for years. My reason for giving is both need and opportunity. At first, I mostly gave to causes that personally affected me or someone I knew, and I typically gave during targeted times of the year. As I became more involved in my community, I naturally began to give my time. At first, I volunteered in my daughters' school, for Girl Scouts, and at my church. I was asked to become more involved with each group and I took on more responsibility. As my husband became involved in town soccer, I assisted him with the administrative aspects of his role as coach. In recent years, I have been approached by various organizations to participate on their boards of directors. This brought an entirely new element to giving. I not only provided financial and volunteer support, but I also reached out to friends and family to bring awareness to the cause.

In 2004, I launched my organizing business which gave me even more opportunity to give. I now had products and services that could be donated as door prizes and auction items, providing vehicles for the organizations to earn money. As awareness grew, additional groups approached me to donate to their cause. I found this to be an easy way to become involved with different organizations from those I had been used to. The type of giving I provide includes gift certificates for my services, the donation of products related to my business industry, and volunteer service as a committee member or chairperson. This involvement often leads to serving as a board member for a non-profit group. Many times I have provided educational workshops to local libraries, home day care groups, and other home-based businesses on the topic of organizing. This type of giving provides me the greatest reward since I am transferring knowledge that I have gained over the years to others who need it. The topics range from organizational tips on paper and time management, to organizing a small business. I also speak to targeted audiences on life transitions such as corporate moves and downsizing seniors.

Each January, I volunteer many hours to educate the general public throughout the state on organizing. This past year, my topic was estate organizing and managing important life transitions. This topic is near and dear to me and has become a specialty interest area of my business. Too often, I hear that seniors are passing on without having an opportunity to properly disperse their personal belongings or gift them to loved ones. Many times it is much too late when the conversations begin regarding what to do with grandma's silver tea set or who should receive the family photos stored in a box in the attic. There are valuable stories being left untold and special memories being discarded too abruptly. My specialty has allowed me to share with my clients (often the adult children of the homeowners) ways in which belongings can be reused by others and recycled through charitable giving to those in need, rather that being discarded into our landfills.

The importance of controlling waste is one that I educate my clients on regularly and I always offer multiple names of charities based on their area of interest. I encourage my clients to consider old cell phones, small furnishings, and twin sheet sets as donations for battered women's shelters. This allows them to furnish small apartments they live in as safe havens and also gives them the ability to phone for help in emergency situations. Old towels and rags are warmly welcomed at animal shelters to use for bedding. Vintage clothing and accessories are often desired by theater groups for their costume shops. Shoes and clothing in any condition are needed for consumers with limited income and often get transported to Third World countries. Often people are uneasy donating personal effects that are worn or even torn; however, these items are desperately needed in certain areas of the world. Once clients are aware of this, it often gives them great satisfaction and pride to donate their items.

As a member of the National Association of Professional Organizers (NAPO), I participate in an annual initiative known nationally as GO Month, or Get Organized Month. The purpose of this month-long event is to educate the public on the industry of professional organizing. I first volunteered for this event 4 years ago to help promote my business in specific geographical areas. Over time, I have come to truly enjoy the public speaking venue and the question and answer audience participation portion of the presentation. When I provide space saving tips or organizing advice to someone struggling with everyday tasks, or guidance to someone dealing with the issues surrounding an aging loved one, I feel a great sense of accomplishment.

In April 2008, I was given the great honor of participating on a 7-person panel in Reno, Nevada at the NAPO annual conference. In attendance were over 600 professional organizers from around the country, mostly new to the industry, but many seasoned organizers as well who run successful organizing businesses. Following my participation on the panel, I was astonished to hear that my colleagues considered me an expert in my field. Had I not volunteered my time, I might never have known this.

Locally, I attended monthly meetings for the Connecticut chapter of NAPO and served on a number of committees. I chaired the recognitions committee, which allowed me to recognize numerous members with a host of awards. I also took great pride in greeting guests and members at the start of many meetings, serving as a buddy for the first-timers, introducing them to others, and making them feel welcome. I was recognized twice as Volunteer of the Month. This particular group is made up of more than 60 business owners who volunteer their time specifically for the industry of Professional Organizing.

Weekly, I participate in a business networking group as a means to enhance business referrals among the members. For the past 3 years, I have served in a volunteer position on the leadership team of this group. It is my belief that my time is recognized and appreciated by my colleagues, which entices them to give of their time as well. The volunteerism I provide allows the group to recognize great achievements, such as business ventures that reach the community through educational seminars on a variety of topics. This group recently made a monetary donation to a local organization allowing it to purchase the equivalent of $1,500 worth of food for their pantry.

When I initially started my business, I had an abundance of free time to network and volunteer my time. At first, this started as a means of getting my new business recognized in the community, but quickly became a rewarding way to support local communities. As I started to volunteer more, I also became recognized as a person willing to share ideas for the good of the cause. I was asked to serve on various boards of directors and was given more responsibility over time. I remember from my early days of volunteerism that empowering others was the best way to achieve greater results, so I began to give advice on improving fundraising events which later provided greater profits for the organization. I also encouraged others from the community to get involved. I suggested they start small by serving on a committee and over time asked them to chair that committee or serve on a board which allowed them to impact decisions. With volunteerism comes recognition, and many times this is the initial reason businesses and individuals provide giving. It is certainly necessary for small business owners to become recognized for their giving, but for me, the greatest satisfaction comes in creating change for the greater good of the organization. This reward is exponentially satisfying.

Soon enough, I realized I possessed the ability to enhance an organization's success through my efforts. I became an advocate for membership growth, speaking with anyone I felt could benefit from involvement. As a board member for various non-profit groups, I reached out to my colleagues for financial support and other forms of giving. Today, I serve as the president for my town's business association, with a mission to bring greater awareness to the community of the businesses and civic organizations that support the community. I believe it is this kind of involvement that forms great communities. My community is one in which is home to a remarkable food pantry serving dozens of needy families from town, church groups that provide countless outreach programs and support for our community and neighboring communities, and an incredible community of volunteers, to name a few. Giving, I believe, is contagious, and when a person's heart is opened to a cause, the possibilities for achieving greatness are endless.

When I first launched my business, I joined the local Chamber of Commerce. I was provided with invaluable advice and guidance that I will always cherish. I attended many Chamber events where I soon began to volunteer, as thanks for the valuable business advice I was given. The Chamber in which I am involved hosts a number of community events each year and I proudly participate and volunteer my time whenever possible. I enjoy being associated with successful organizations that give to the community.

I also feel strongly about educating our youth and volunteer each year at our high school's career fair. At this event, students ask questions about forming a business and the education required to be successful. By providing answers to their questions and asking them what draws them to a specific career, I learn a great deal about what motivates them. Sharing my own personal experiences is yet another rewarding type of giving.

In addition to the career fair, our high school is always in need of volunteers at assemblies and school concerts. My business has supported the music boosters program by providing funding for the event program, donating products to be used for raffles, and volunteering time prior to the start of the event. I also attend meetings when possible as a representative of the business community.

Most recently, I began another form of giving that I never felt possible. I was able to use my business to support my giving. I am currently running a fundraiser to support a special person in need. The recipient is the most generous person I know on this earth. She has provided countless hours of charitable activities over the 19 years I have known her, supporting needy families, school children, disabled individuals and so many other groups. As the need exists, she finds new and creative ways to support the cause. All along, she has been suffering as her own struggles escalated. I learned of personal loss, injuries, financial troubles, business issues, motor vehicle accidents, and family issues. I soon realized the situation was of a dire nature. I formulated a way to create immediate cash flow for her to support her daily needs. I contacted business clients and acquaintances for support. I am offering organizing products for sale at discounted prices to entice consumers to participate. Once they learned of the cause, the discount didn't matter. People came forward with monetary donations and words of hope. The response has been overwhelming and the well wishes have been incredibly inspiring. I am learning a great deal from this experience and am happy to report renewed hope for my friend. The years of giving came back to her in her time of need, supporting my belief that there is good in all of us.

For many years, I belonged to an organization that taught business etiquette and interviewing skills and provided attire for high-risk youths and disadvantaged men. The organization, Clothes Make the Man, is based in Connecticut and was founded in 2003. While most of my volunteerism and financial support occurred far from headquarters, one day I was asked to provide assistance with interviewing and outfitting new clients. I was apprehensive at first, knowing the history of some of the clients, but decided to put my concerns aside for the good of the cause. My one-hour appointment was with a middle-aged man being measured for a business suit and being prepped for an upcoming interview. I recall assisting the man in trying on jackets to fit his build, followed by choosing the right tie to complement his suit. There was awkwardness when I assisted the client with tying his tie and coaching him on how to act during the interview. When the man was fully outfitted and his tie properly tied, he stood in front of the mirror with confidence he didn't have one hour earlier. A short time following this appointment, three young men arrived for their group appointment. They were at-risk youths from the community preparing for a job fair. After coaching them on cell phone usage and making eye contact, we proceeded to fit each of them for business suits. Two had never before worn a suit and one had only worn one for the funeral of a friend. None of the three had ever before tied a necktie. My eyes were opened to a world I didn't know but I was proud to make a small difference in their lives that day. The quiet young men that arrived that afternoon left the office laughing and feeling good about their appearances.

I have been afforded many opportunities to give in a multitude of ways over the years and recently implemented a business policy offering discounted workshops to non-profit groups requesting seminars on organizing topics. The greatest issue I face, as the owner of the Organized East of the River, is the inability to respond to all requests. It is for this reason that I continue to educate others and empower people around me.

I have been able to quantify the results of charitable giving as follows:

Volunteerism allows me to meet new people, providing me the opportunity for increased awareness of my business and business referrals. The benefit to the cause is simple in that volunteer hours are free labor needed to run the organization or charitable event.

Financial Support comes in a variety of forms. For instance, sponsoring an event gains the business public awareness through print advertising and marketing of the event. Many charitable groups rely on their boards of directors to personally provide financial support or solicit financial support from business colleagues and associates. A civic organization cannot provide basic administrative duties without the financial support of others through charitable giving.

In-Kind Donations are most popular in that they require less out-of-pocket cost than outright cash giving and little to no time to implement. These items are usually products from the business donated to the organization to use for raffle prizes and auction items. The proceeds from the sales of raffle tickets usually far outweigh the wholesale cost of the item donated, making this a very desirable way to raise funds for an organization.

Personally, my business has benefited in the following ways from charitable giving over the years:

1. Community awareness of the business in the community through added exposure resulting from giving.
2. Support from others who experience the kindness and recognize the business as a force in the community.
3. Confidence from the community in you as a person, and therefore in you as a business owner.
4. Recognition from local politicians, gaining added support with community issues as they arise.
5. Recognition from fellow business owners, gaining confidence in making business-to-business referrals.
6. Respect from others who support your cause.
7. A voice in important matters and the ability to effect change when needed.
8. Making a difference in the lives of others.
9. Personal satisfaction being involved in the good of the cause.

Clearly, for me, there is no question that giving provides me personally with balance and a great deal of satisfaction. For my business, it identifies who I am, gives me credibility as a business owner, and allows others to trust in me. This is an incredibly important value to have in my business as I am often entrusted with personal belongings and expected to guide clients through difficult processes. While I believe giving is a personal and often private choice, I encourage business owners to consider the opportunities around them.

— **Donna V. Finocchiaro,** owner, Organized East of the River, Marlborough, CT

Organized East of the River is a Professional Organizing company specializing in managing life's important transitions. As an industry expert, Donna and her team assists families with upsizing, downsizing, whole house clear-outs, corporate moves and staging homes for sale. The services offered include face to face consultations, providing industry resources, written reports on actionable items, and hands-on organizing services. Often times, organizing products are used to enhance the area and improve the functionality of the space. Donna has a variety of resources to offer the latest in organizing products.

Contact Information

www.organizedeast.com

Afterword

"I expect to pass through life but once. If, therefore, there can be any kindness I can show, or any good thing I can do to any fellow human being, let me do it now, and not defer it or neglect it, as I shall not pass this way again." —William Penn

Out of inspiration comes change. Out of change comes something better. This is exactly how a giving program begins and affects the world, lives and communities. It starts with the desire and inspiration to champion a cause. What is your cause? Do you know? Was a thought jogged in your mind while reading this book? Did you write a few notes or ideas down on a sticky? Did you post that sticky by your computer with the notion you will get to it later? Are you thinking you'll need to wait until you have more time or more money to start a giving program for your business?

Keep in mind, it's about the impact you make with your giving; not about how much you have to give. The most effective giving program is the one that leverages your time, cash, and knowledge, is guided by your core values and is planned with a strategy that allows for contingencies. At certain times in your business and throughout a year, your giving will fluctuate depending on the cycles of your business, but your message and purpose remain constants. The message, purpose and plan are the most important elements for a giving program to withstand hard economic times, and it will build your reputation as a business that stands for something beyond the balance sheet.

There are five success strategies to building a business giving program:

1. Authentic: Your giving story and message are true to your core values, not someone else's.

2. Aligned: Your cause(s) are aligned with what is important to you and your business, not with what the most popular color awareness ribbon is.
3. Asset conscious: Your asset strengths define how you give and can set you apart from others. Think beyond the checkbook approach.
4. Anchored: Your giving program is a reflection of your unwavering, steadfast commitment to solving social issues, and your business is energized by it.
4. Action: Give and give consistently. Do not take your eye off what you see possible for the world.

When it comes to taking action that makes a change toward something better, there is no better time than now. In the words of William Penn, "Let me do it *now* and not defer or neglect it…" Face it, we do what is important to us. As the stories in this book reflect, giving is important to each of these business owners. Their charitable giving program is an integral part of business and their giving influences decisions and the connections they make with customers and community.

I hope you made a connection with the stories in this book and that at least one inspired you to want to start a business giving program. You can give this book to a partner, an employee, or anyone else in your business to read. Talk about it, brainstorm over ideas, and make a decision to pursue something good, to do good, and experience the joy and rewards you receive through giving back. The possibilities for giving are endless.

If the task of starting a business giving program leaves you feeling as if you don't know where or how to start, then start small. But just start, *now.*

About Maggie F. Keenan, Ed.D.

Maggie F. Keenan, Ed.D. has never been the kind of business owner or long distance runner that is content being behind the leader. Instead, Maggie wakes up every morning driven by the desire to make a difference in the world, to inspire others to do the same, and to get her miles in. She is the Owner and Chief Giving Strategist of givingadvice™, dedicated to providing strategic philanthropy services to business.

Maggie's discipline and dedication motivated her to excel as a competitive long-distance runner. The early mornings runs prepare her to stay focused on her goals. But, Maggie's focus is no longer on competitive running. Instead it's on her vision to make a profound difference in the world. A passionate advocate in business philanthropy, Maggie has made a difference over the last 15 years for both her clients and the causes they care about the most. She is convinced we are living in one of the most dynamic yet turbulent times, with great disparities in the world. Maggie sees this as an incredible opportunity for change, one in which businesses can have an important part. Philanthropy when integrated as a core business strategy has a direct impact on the business and the world.

In her work with small businesses owners and solo entrepreneurs through her Six Step Giving IMPACT Strategy™ model, Maggie provides a blueprint and strategy unique for each client. Her clients are most attracted by her passion and vision for what she sees possible for their contribution to the world. With an uncanny ability to connect ideas, people, and causes, she sees opportunities all around for anyone that desires to be a force for change.

Maggie lives and works in Savannah, Georgia. She holds a Doctorate from the University of Georgia and is a graduate of Virginia Commonwealth University and Temple University. She's a member of the Inaugural Class of the Robert Hull Leadership Fellow of Southeastern Council of Foundations, and a 2000 Savannah Leadership Fellow. She is also the Founder of Savannah Women Connect, a professional business women's network. You can find Maggie running on the beach when she isn't in her office.

For more information on her consulting programs, services and speaking engagements, please contact Maggie at:

Maggie F. Keenan, Ed.D.
Chief Giving Strategist
givingadvice™
P.O. Box 16876
Savannah, GA 31416
Email: info@givingadvicc.com
Main website: www.givingadvice.com
Book website: www.smallbusinessesgivebig.com
Book blog: http://smallbusinessesgivebig.blogspot.com

Share Your Giving Story!

Does your business have a giving back story? Would you like to share your giving story and experience with other small business owners? Then I want to hear from you. Your giving may inspire others to think about making giving an important part of their business — whether they have been in business for six months or six years.

Your story could be featured on my blog, givigsuccess! ezine, or teleclass. Share your story with me at:

- Email: info@givingadvice.com
- Book blog: http://smallbusinessesgivebig.blogspot.com

Stories change hearts and change lives.

An Invitation

givingadvice™ exists to serve community-minded businesses and socially conscious entrepreneurs by providing strategies and resources they need to create a giving program that grows and transforms their business, communities, and the world. Below are resources and services to help you get started.

Small Business Giving Coaching and Consulting

If you want to create a giving program for your business or if you want to enhance an existing one, givingadvice offers coaching and consulting programs. To help you determine the right fit for your business needs, I invite you to contact me for a complimentary 'get acquainted' session by sending an email to **info@givingadvice.com**.

Five Ways a Giving Program Can Increase Your Business's Value

A giving program can have a powerful and positive impact on your business. In this special report, you learn the top five ways businesses grow and gain by giving back. The report is free when you sign up for the **givingsuccess!™** ezine.

givingsuccess!™ ezine

givingsuccess! is a free monthly online newsletter. You receive valuable tips, strategies and resources to help you build, manage and grow your business giving program. Visit **www.givingadvice.com** to sign up.

www.ingramcontent.com/pod-product-compliance
Lightning Source LLC
LaVergne TN
LVHW020644100826
845148LV00012B/2331

* 9 7 8 0 9 7 9 6 7 4 5 5 6 *